C
T
S
P9-CQH-498

Volumes in The New
Church's Teaching Series

The Anglican Vision
James E. Griffiss

Opening the Bible
Roger Ferlo

Engaging the Word
Michael Johnston

The Practice of Prayer
Margaret Guenther

Living With History
Fredrica Harris Thompsett

Early Christian Traditions
Rebecca Lyman

Opening the Prayer Book
Jeffrey Lee

Mysteries of Faith
Mark McIntosh

Ethics After Easter
Stephen Holmgren

Christian Social Witness
Harold T. Lewis

Horizons of Mission
Titus Presler

A Theology of Worship
Louis Weil

Christian Wholeness
Martin L. Smith, SSJE

Horizons of Mission

The New
Church's Teaching Series,
Volume 11

Horizons
of Mission

Titus Presler

COWLEY PUBLICATIONS
Cambridge · Boston
Massachusetts

The title *The Church's Teaching Series* is used by permission of the Domestic and Foreign Missionary Society. Use of the series title does not constitute the Society's endorsement of the content of the work.

Published in the United States of America by Cowley Publications, a division of the Society of St. John the Evangelist. No portion of this book may be reproduced, stored in or introduced into a retrieval system, or transmitted, in any form or by any means—including photocopying—without the prior written permission of Cowley Publications, except in the case of brief quotations embedded in critical articles and reviews.

Library of Congress Cataloging-in-Publication Data:
Presler, Titus Leonard.
    Horizons of mission / by Titus L. Presler.
       p. cm. — (The new church's teaching series; v. 11)
    Includes bibliographical references.
    ISBN 1-56101-190-8 (alk. paper)
    1. Anglican Communion—Missions. 2. Missions—Theory.
    I. Title. II. Series.
BV2500 .P74 2001
266'.3—dc21   200128199

Cynthia Shattuck, editor; Vicki Black, copyeditor and designer.
Cover art: The Olive Trees (1889), Vincent Van Gogh

Scripture quotations are taken from *The New Revised Standard Version* of the Bible, © 1989, by the Division of Christian Education of the National Council of the Churches of Christ in the United States of America. Used by permission.

This book was printed by Transcontinental Printing in Canada on recycled, acid-free paper.

Cowley Publications
28 Temple Place • *Boston, Massachusetts 02111*
800-225-1534 • *www.cowley.org*

Table of Contents

The New Church's Teaching Series

Almost fifty years ago a series for the Episcopal Church called The Church's Teaching was launched with the publication of Robert Dentan's *The Holy Scriptures* in 1949. Again in the 1970s the church commissioned another church's teaching series for the next generation of Anglicans. Originally the series was part of an effort to give the growing postwar churches a sense of Anglican identity: what Anglicans share with the larger Christian community and what makes them distinctive within it. During that seemingly more tranquil era it may have been easier to reach a consensus and to speak authoritatively. Now, at the end of the twentieth century, consensus and authority are more difficult; there is considerably more diversity of belief and practice within the churches today, and more people than ever who have never been introduced to the church at all.

The books in this new teaching series for the Episcopal Church attempt to encourage and respond to the times and to the challenges that will usher out the old century and bring in the new. This new series differs from the previous two in significant ways: it has no official status, claims no special authority, speaks in a personal voice, and comes not out of committees but from scholars and pastors meeting and talking informally together. It assumes a different readership: adults who are not "cradle Anglicans," but who come from other religious traditions or from no tradition at all, and who want to know what Anglicanism has to offer.

As the series editor I want to thank E. Allen Kelley, former president of Morehouse Publishing, for initially inviting me to bring together a group of teachers and pastors who could write with learning and conviction about their faith. I am grateful both to him and to Morehouse for participating in the early development of the series.

Since those initial conversations there have been changes in the series itself, but its basic purpose has remained: to explore the themes of the Christian life through Holy Scripture, historical and contemporary theology, worship, spirituality, and social witness. It is our hope that all readers, Anglicans and otherwise, will find the books an aid in their continuing growth into Christ.

James E. Griffiss
Series Editor

Acknowledgments

A s this book is offered into the community of mission that is the church, I am grateful to communities of people from whom I have learned and who have offered their enthusiasm to the project.

Embracing global engagement, St. Peter's Church in Cambridge, Massachusetts, where I am rector, has become a significant mission community in local outreach, sending missionaries, advocating for Jubilee 2000, and participating in mission councils. I am grateful to the entire congregation and especially to Wardens Lois Bennett and Frank Smith and Wider Mission Co-Chairs Douglas and Sallie Craig Huber for being companions in mission with me.

My many colleagues in the Episcopal Partnership for Global Mission have taught me a great deal about commitment and vision in the diverse modes of mission they pursue. I am especially grateful to Edwina Thomas of Sharing of Ministries Abroad, Tom Prichard of the South American Missionary Society, Jackie Kraus of the United Thank Offering and the Diocese of Chicago, Tad de Bordenave of Anglican Frontier Missions, Sandi McPhee of the Kiyosato Educational Experiment Project and the Diocese of Chicago, and Ian Douglas of the Episcopal Divinity School.

The Volunteers for Mission Committee of the Diocese of Massachusetts has been a context for developing a theology and strategy for mission sending and receiving. I am grateful to my colleagues Barbara Ramsey, Louis Pitt, Homer McCue, Sallie Craig Huber, Melvena Green, Tom Callard, and the late Paul Dettman. I am grateful to my colleagues on the Standing Commission on World Mission for helping to catalyze my thinking about world mission in the Episcopal Church and the Anglican Communion.

I am grateful to Gaul Theological College in Harare, Harvard Divinity School, and the General Theological Seminary for their teaching invitations and to the students who interacted with ideas presented in this book. Outgoing missionaries in the ecumenical Mission Personnel Orientation have offered valuable insight, and I am especially grateful to Liz and Lin Parsons and Ann Makarias, missionaries from St. Peter's.

There are more people than I can name in Zimbabwe who have shaped not only my mission thinking but my experience of God through our companionship in mission over twenty years. For all of them I am very thankful. Editors Cynthia Shattuck and Vicki Black have been a joy to work with at Cowley Publications, and I thank them for their encouragement and insight.

My wife Jane Butterfield is a mission companion both in our African experiences and in the mission advocacy we share in the Episcopal Church. I am deeply grateful for her support and enthusiasm throughout the germinating and blossoming of this project. Our daughters Emma and Charlotte and sons Titus and Amos have likewise been wonderfully supportive, and I thank them.

I dedicate this book to my parents, Henry Hughes Presler (1909-1998) and Marion Anders Presler, who served as missionaries in India from 1937 to 1972. In later years I have realized that the very names they gave me turn out to have prefigured my mission engagements: Titus, after both the apostle Paul's missioner on Crete and Murray Titus, a missionary to India and scholar of Islam; and Leonard, after the Leonard Theological College in Jabalpur. My parents lived a mission stance that was credible and compelling, inquiring and witnessing. I thank God for them.

Chapter One

Dilemma and Discernment in Mission Today

It was while sitting on a dormitory bunk bed with my friends at the age of eight that I had the first experience I remember of trying to sort out what Christian mission is. As children of missionaries in India, we attended a boarding school in the Himalaya Mountains, a wonderful environment for years of trekking and interacting with Indian people and their cultures. That year, my friends and I were so devout that once a week we had our own afterschool Bible study back in the dorm.

On this particular day we were talking about what our parents did. One boy's parents pastored a Baptist congregation in a Bengali village near Calcutta, and he described the evangelistic outreach through which villagers were becoming Christians and the congregation was growing. In their rural development work in central India, another boy's Mennonite parents dug wells in dry villages, installed electric generators, and taught farming techniques. Another boy's Presbyterian parents headed a technical training college in north India, where it was clear that the budding mechanics and electricians were also being nurtured as Christian leaders.

"I wish my parents would get on with some *real* missionary work," I said after listening to my friends. "I can't figure it out. My father seems to spend all his time visiting Hindu temples and talking with the priests and writing down what they say. He's got a whole bunch of students doing the same thing, and sometimes they go with him. And then there's an office of secretaries typing up the notes. And my mother's the same way, only she gets excited about Muslim festivals at the top of this hill near Jabalpur, where we live."

I remember the incident so clearly because afterward I felt disloyal about criticizing my parents out loud. The criticism came from the confusion I was feeling about my family's role in the mission enterprise. I was born in India, and throughout my childhood and youth I felt that just *being* in India was a remarkable privilege. Like most children, I accepted my parents' work as part of the landscape of my life, but in this conversation of young theologians I realized that I did not understand how their work as Christian missionaries related to the gospel that was becoming important to me.

In a general way, I knew what my United Methodist parents were doing. Henry and Marion Presler taught at Leonard Theological College, and I understood that meant they were preparing Indians to become pastors of churches. Sometimes their students adopted me as a kind of mascot, and I especially enjoyed listening to the Mar Thoma seminarians from Kerala speak their native Malayalam, so much more mellifluous than the Hindi I knew. I could not attend the classes my parents taught, so what I was reacting to with my friends was the apparently unending research, because I *could* see that. I had accompanied my sociologist father on research outings and listened as he talked with priests and devotees about their beliefs and practices, the configurations of images in the temples, and so forth. I climbed with my mother the many steps of Madan Mahal and visited the shrines at the top, where she studied Islam as a psychologist of religion. As a family we went to the Hindu festivals, or *melas*, partly as fun outings, but also partly for the research. We might end up talking with a wandering mendicant, or *sadhu*, who had buried himself up to the neck in the ground in devotion to Shiva or Krishna.

The research was worthwhile in itself—I was enough of a student to know that, even at eight. The questions I shared with my friends were different. What did all this have to do with the gospel? Didn't the Hindus, Muslims, Jains, and Parsis my parents were talking with need to hear about Jesus? How could my parents be real missionaries if they weren't doing evangelism? Wasn't it important to establish congregations and make sure they grew? In the horrifying poverty of India, shouldn't missionaries be helping people with the practical goals they might have for their lives—clean water, healthy children, electrical power, good schools, marketable skills?

My friends and I had our conversation in the late 1950s. Even though we were children, we were touching on questions of Christian world mission that became urgent for all churches after World War II, issues we are still wrestling with as the twenty-first century opens:

- The relationship between proclaiming the gospel and trying to understand other religions.

• The relationship between building congregations and helping people in the practical ways that are often called "development."

• The relationship between "doing *for*" other people and "working *with*" them in partnerships that fulfill *their* agenda rather than our own.

The horizons this book explores are the international, global horizons of the church's mission. This chapter will plow the ground of dilemmas that individuals, parishes, and dioceses experience as they engage the global dimension of mission. Yet mission is an aspect of Christian living that is broader than world mission alone, and we must first explore that more general reality of mission in the church's life.

～ Identity, Purpose, and Function

Our Himalayan conversation highlights how mission questions are always questions of identity, purpose, and function: Who are we? What are our goals? What are we supposed to be doing? This is true of all the places where the word "mission" is used—in business, education, and diplomacy, as well as in the churches. "Mission statements" have become a principal strategy of organizational renewal since the late twentieth century. Typically, a company or nonprofit agency hires a consultant to convene its staff for a weekend retreat, where participants share their joys and frustrations and work intensively to craft a statement that articulates their purpose as an organization.

The historic association of the word "mission" with "doing good" of some kind means that the mission-statement exercise prompts even for-profit corporations to envision their identity, purpose, and function altruistically as well as economically. Marketing strategy plays a role, of course, but there is at least the rhetoric of wanting to do something for others as well as to make a profit for owners and shareholders. For instance, Ben & Jerry's, the ice cream company, worked out its mission statement in three parts— Product, Economic, and Social—that are reproduced in large and brightly colored lettering above the crowds that throng the visitors' center at its Vermont factory. The social mission is:

> To operate the company in a way that actively recognizes the central role that business plays in the structure of society in initiating innovative ways to improve the quality of life of a broad community: local, national and international.

The company says it implements its social mission through assisting a number of groups, including environmentalists around Lake Champlain, vanilla farmers in Costa Rica, summer campers in California, and coffee growers in Mexico. Among the mission statements of nonprofit organizations, the YMCA's is illustrative: "To put Christian principles into practice through programs that build healthy spirit, mind, and body for all."

It is for good reason that the word "mission" stimulates organizations and individuals to think about their identity, purpose, and function. Its root is the Latin verb *mittere*, which means "to send," and it is easy to see the resemblance between one of its forms, *missum*, which means "I have been sent," and our English word "mission." Mission, therefore, has to do with sending and being sent, which raises the question of what one is being sent to do. The old American television show "Mission Impossible" opened with secret agents listening to a tape recording of their boss telling them what their next daunting assignment was, after which the tape would self-destruct.

However impossible their errand might seem, they were nevertheless being *sent* to carry it out. Embassies and consulates of a government in other countries are often called "missions" because they are staffed by diplomats *sent* to represent officially the interests of their nation. In wartime, negotiators are often *sent* on "peace missions." Astronauts fly on "space missions" because they are *sent* to explore interplanetary space.

Who are we? What is our purpose? How are we to function? These are universal questions about human existence, asked in one way or another by all people in all times and places. When we include the dimension of sending and being sent they become *mission* questions: Who are we sent to be? What purpose are we sent to carry out? How are we to function on that errand? For religious people, the questions entail the reality of God, not just as one of many factors in the situation, but as the ultimate frame of reference. God is the sender, we are the sent ones. So what has God sent us to be? What is God's purpose in sending us? What does God seek to accomplish through us in the world?

∿ The Church's Mission
When we look to scripture, we see that the Bible is full of sending and being sent. "So come," God says to Moses at the burning bush, "I will send you to Pharaoh to bring my people, the Israelites, out of Egypt" (Exodus 3:10). Isaiah's temple vision is all about sending: "Then I heard the voice of the Lord saying, 'Whom shall I send, and who will go for us?' And I said, 'Here am I; send me!'" (Isaiah 6:8). Being sent was the heart of being a disciple of Jesus: "Jesus called the twelve together and gave them power and authority over all demons and to cure diseases, and he sent them out to proclaim the kingdom of God and to

heal" (Luke 9:1-2). That sending echoed Jesus' own experience of being sent by God: "As the Father has sent me, so I send you" (John 20:21). Sending was also central in the coming of the Holy Spirit as Jesus promised, "The Advocate, the Holy Spirit, whom the Father will send in my name, will teach you every-thing, and remind you of all that I have said to you" (John 14:26).

"What is the mission of the Church?" asks the Catechism in the Episcopal Church's *Book of Common Prayer* (BCP 855). It answers that question by sum-marizing all this sending and being sent in one sen-tence: "The mission of the Church is to restore all people to unity with God and each other in Christ." Unity is so often cited as a social ideal or a political goal that it can seem innocuous and even trivial as a concept. Unity in the Bible and the Catechism, howev-er, is not a bland consensus that suppresses diversity, nor does it imply merging people and things into a single, homogenized entity. Rather, the biblical writers have in mind the vital and creative community with God and one another for which we were made and which we see in the Garden of Eden. Unity of purpose amid a diversity of being is the vision, realized through harmonious relationships among many kinds of living beings and individuals. Such a restora-tion is the mission of the church, says the Catechism. It is what the church is sent to bring about.

How? is the natural rejoinder, when our mission is set forth as a task both so general and so large, even grandiose. In fact, that is the Catechism's next ques-tion: "How does the Church pursue its mission?" Its answer: "The Church pursues its mission as it prays and worships, proclaims the Gospel, and promotes justice, peace, and love." That is a reassuring state-ment of the church's mission, because it includes the diversity of activities we experience in the church's life. Praying as well as proclaiming is part of the church's mission, spirituality as well as evangelism, being as well as doing. Proclaiming the gospel through preaching and congregational life is certainly prominent in the church's mission, but so must be our engagement in practical struggles to bring about justice and peace in the world, whether locally or globally. All these are ways of restoring people to unity with God, with one another, and with all creation in Christ.

Looking at the church's mission in this way helps us to see that some of the dilemmas about mission we think we are facing may be false. We may think we are facing an *either-or* choice when, in fact, it is a case of *both-and*. We may not need to choose, for instance, *either* evangelism *or* social justice, but may be called to embrace *both*. The good news might be expressed through a justice ministry; an evangelistic conversation might suggest an affordable-housing initiative; meals with the homeless might lead to offering eucharist. Particular individuals and communities have particular gifts and callings, so inevitably we all have distinct emphases. No community can do everything, so each congregation tends to major in a few areas of mission, but collectively the entire church is carrying out the whole mission of God, whether through the Episcopal Church in the United States, the Anglican Church of Canada, the Church of England, the worldwide Anglican Communion, or the global Christian community. A good test or criterion of any initiative is whether it fulfills the Catechism's mission statement. Does this particular initiative help restore people to unity with God and each other in Christ? Or does it distract us from that central mission—or even harm our efforts to restore such community?

Not all of this was clear to me at age eight, but as my views became more comprehensive I began to realize that my parents' grassroots inquiry with people of other religions and the publications that came from it were a unique contribution to understanding popular religion in India. Forums they organized on religious topics at the University of Jabalpur were, for that time and even now, an unusual venture in interfaith dialogue. For seminary students who came from ghetto-like Christian communities in India, field research about the major religions that surrounded them was a crucial breakthrough that enabled them to understand the religious environment of their future ministries. So the teaching these two missionaries offered was not beside the point of missionary work. It was, instead, an essential contribution to the mission task of strengthening indigenous Christian communities in their life and leadership in the world. Understanding such breadth and diversity in world mission helped to inform my own later and now ongoing work in Africa.

What has God sent us to be? What is God's purpose in sending us? What does God seek to accomplish through us in the world? These are central mission questions for all Christian communities. These are questions that Episcopal and Anglican congregations should be asking as we seek to discern God's vision for our living and working in the world. The good news in this new century is that Anglican communities throughout the world are asking mission questions more often and more urgently than they have before. Although world mission has been an important Anglican initiative since about 1700, Anglican churches have often been better known for supporting the comfortable, wealthy establishment in their communities and nations rather than for reaching out to human need, whether at home or in the wider world.

⸤ Mission activism is now replacing Anglican complacency, a shift that the church supports daily and weekly in its worship. Just as the current Episcopal Catechism asks mission questions that previous catechisms did not ask, so also the 1979 *Book of Common Prayer* highlights mission in the church's prayer life. The liturgies for Morning, Noonday, and Evening Prayer include collects for mission that range from local to global (BCP 100-01, 107, 124-25). The Great Thanksgiving, which, with the restoration of the Holy Eucharist as the principal service on Sunday morning, is increasingly central in the church's worship, highlights God's mission in the world through Jesus. In Eucharistic Prayer A, for instance, we pray:

> In your infinite love you made us for yourself; and, when we had fallen into sin and become subject to evil and death, you, in your mercy, sent Jesus Christ, your only and eternal Son, to share our human nature, to live and die as one of us, to reconcile us to you, the God and Father of all. (BCP 362)

As Jesus was sent into the world, we ask God at the end of the eucharist to *send* us into the world:

> Send us now into the world in peace, and grant us strength and courage to love and serve you with gladness and singleness of heart; through Christ our Lord. (BCP 365)

The prayer book includes a liturgy for commissioning persons for Christian service (BCP 420-21), and the ordination liturgies for bishops, priests, and deacons highlight the mission they are to carry out. The bishop's charge to a deacon ordinand is illustrative:

> In the name of Jesus Christ, you are to serve all
> people, particularly the poor, the weak, the sick,
> and the lonely.... You are to make Christ and
> his redemptive love known, by your word and
> example, to those among whom you live, and
> work, and worship. You are to interpret to the
> Church the needs, concerns, and hopes of the
> world. (BCP 543)

The support that our worship offers for mission fulfills the Anglican emphasis on the connection between
our praying and our believing. "The rule of praying is
the rule of believing," goes the adage (*lex orandi lex
credendi* in the Latin original), meaning that our theology is shaped by our experience of God in prayer. As
our praying joins God's initiative in mission, we
become more committed to mission, and the rule of
praying becomes the rule not only for believing but
for acting as well.

The Baptismal Covenant (BCP 304-05) that the
baptized members of the congregation renew together
at every baptism is regarded increasingly as a commissioning or mission-sending for all who are present, and the mission statements that congregations
and dioceses develop are often based on that covenant,
as well as on gleanings from scripture and the
Catechism. Identity, vocation, and mission are three
themes that Presiding Bishop Frank Griswold recently
encouraged Episcopalians to reflect on at the turn of
the centuries: We must "deepen our identity in
Christ,... claim our vocation to be the Body of
Christ," Griswold noted, "and be about Christ's mission," interpreted as the liberating work of jubilee.[1] In
1995 the General Synod of the Anglican Church of
Canada committed itself to "promote and develop
mission, with enthusiasm and prayer, in a manner

which engages the church in circles of partnership, locally, nationally, globally and ecumenically."[2]

Mission urgency is intensifying throughout the Anglican Communion. As part of the Decade of Evangelism (1990-2000), the Anglican Church of Nigeria consecrated nine missionary bishops to offer new witness and strengthen Anglican presence in the predominantly Muslim areas of northern Nigeria.[3] With the creation of nine new dioceses, the task of each bishop was to be a catalyst for conversions and build a diocese from congregations of new Christians. Stirring eloquence and risky struggle to end apartheid in South Africa made Desmond Tutu, former archbishop of Southern Africa, the most widely known and admired Anglican of the twentieth century, and his work, like that of Martin Luther King, Jr., reminded Anglicans that prophetic work for liberation and justice is essential to God's mission in the world. The 1998 Lambeth Conference of Anglican Bishops resolved to "accept the imperative character of our call to mission and evangelism as grounded in the very nature of the God who is revealed to us."[4]

The fact that mission is the touchstone of so many meetings, statements, sermons, and initiatives in the church indicates a growing awareness among Anglicans that it is not enough simply to exist as an institution or even as a Christian community, let alone as an isolated Christian, if we are to be faithful to God. Rather, being a gospel person and a gospel community means recognizing that the God who is at work in the world sends God's people to join in that work. In short, being a Christian means being on mission. If one knows God through Jesus Christ in the power of the Holy Spirit—which is one definition of being a Christian—one cannot help participating in God's work in the world. Refusing to be a part of

God's work actually raises the question of whether one truly knows God. As Jesus said, "If you love me, you will keep my commandments" (John 14:15).

In this way, we see that identity, vocation, and mission for Christians are not three separate realities, but are mutually dependent. Christian identity is realized through Christian mission. Mission defines and fulfills identity. Vocation, a word derived from the Latin verb *vocare*, "to call," is the calling every Christian has both to be with God and to carry out God's mission. We can see all this as a theological expression of the relationship between being and doing, living and working. One's being is only partly separable from one's doing, for just as our doing is grounded in our being, our being is realized through our doing. Our doing expresses who we are, but we also *discover* who we are through our doing. Just that intimate is the relationship between Christian identity and Christian mission. As the Swiss theologian Emil Brunner is reputed to have said, "The church exists by mission as fire exists by burning."

◈ A Mission of Transformation
After my ordination I was, like many curates, asked to coordinate youth ministry in the suburban parish I served north of Boston. We bobbed for apples, discussed sex, drugs, and alcohol, rode hay wagons, studied the Bible, prayed together. The group was large, lively, and apparently successful, but it seemed to me that the gospel was not reaching the kids in a way that was going to make a difference in the people they grew up to be. We then organized a summer mission among poor and elderly people in Appalachia. We read Robert Coles's *Children of Crisis* aloud and raised money with car washes and rockathons, but an "infotainment" atmosphere persisted right up to driving

into North Fork in the hollows of West Virginia. The kids gazed out the van windows at the rundown houses they were going to be fixing up, and they grew very quiet. Their ten days there still had a healthy dose of fun, but as they engaged with the people they were helping and prayed and studied together daily they had experiences of Christ that transformed them—for the rest of their lives. Their *being* was transformed by what they *did* in reaching beyond themselves. That is the mystery of responding to God's call to mission.

Such transformation can occur in the lives of entire communities. St. Peter's Episcopal Church in Cambridge, Massachusetts, was a parish concerned about its survival when my wife and I joined it as pastors. Like many city parishes, it had been declining steadily since World War II, so the congregation was asking, "Will we survive? How can we pay the bills? How can we attract more people so that we can make it?" It was clear, however, that asking survival questions was a recipe for not surviving. The questions that needed asking were mission questions: What is God calling us to be and do? How is God moving to restore people to unity with God and one another? How is God calling us to serve the people of Cambridge's Central Square, where many are poor, many are recent immigrants, and crime levels are high? How can we offer community to local people who feel alone and alienated? Without quite realizing it, these were questions the parishioners were longing to hear, and when we asked the questions a new vision for being church began to take hold. The parish engaged community children through an afterschool ministry, immigrants through English as a second language, the marginalized through a meals-in-community outreach, and the general public through a coffee house. St. Peter's developed a global ministry that supports missionaries, took sixty people on pilgrimage to the Bernard Mizeki Festival in Zimbabwe, and promotes jubilee debt cancellation. Survival was soon a non-issue as the liturgy came alive, prayer groups met, and welcome brunches filled up with newcomers. As a suburban youth group was changed by mission, now an urban parish was transformed as it responded to God's mission call.

"Well and good," you might respond, "but we have questions about *world* mission, about mission in its *global* dimension." In fact, questions about global mission abound today. There is an historical irony here. Episcopalians and Anglicans a few generations ago considered mission mainly as a global initiative, and they had relatively few questions about it. The word "mission" was sometimes used for small congregations that needed diocesan help and for special initiatives, such as a "city mission." Generally, however, "mission" meant world mission, which was taken for granted as a good thing, and missionaries were celebrated as they left North America and Europe to serve in Asia, Africa, and Latin America. The word "mission" today has a very broad meaning, as we have seen, and church people find it useful to reflect on that breadth as it affects personal life and the work of their parishes and dioceses. Moreover, mission as local outreach is widely accepted as an integral fruit of Christian community. What people have questions and doubts about today is *world* mission. Questions run the gamut from theological and cultural to strategic and practical.

∾ Questions of World Mission

The rest of this chapter articulates some of the questions about world mission as they are commonly asked and develops them as a background for the rest of the book. While some initial responses are sketched in this chapter, the book as a whole is designed to respond to them more fully. So what are some of those questions?

∿ *If mission is everything a congregation does, as expressed in a "mission statement," what is the basis for thinking that mission involves reaching other people or traveling to other places?*

This is an important question for congregations and for the church in general as we rescue the word "mission" from its almost exclusive association with world mission and consider the breadth of what God is calling us to undertake. The popularity of the mission-statement exercise has corrected a longstanding impression that mission means going to other countries, fullstop. If the previous usage was too narrow, however, there is now the danger that the word "mission" becomes so broad that it loses any sense of sending and being sent to engage someone or someplace beyond who and where we already are. Prayer and worship are certainly part of the church's mission, as the Catechism says, but most people probably would not consider a parish that offered a Sunday liturgy and nothing else to be a mission-activist parish. This illustrates the fact that the meaning of the word "mission" has a persistent and irreducible element of reaching beyond where we already are. "Outreach" is the term that many congregations use to designate that aspect of their mission, and for many it functions as a synonym for mission.

"Mission" then has two senses in the church's life. Broadly, it encompasses all that God asks us to be and do. Included in that general definition is a narrower ..

∞

sense in which we are on mission when we respond to God's call to move beyond who we are and engage someone who is different from ourselves. That sounds abstract, but it is the most general way of expressing the fundamental mission impulse that takes us beyond what we know and moves us to cross frontiers into the new and unfamiliar. The borders that mission takes us over may be social or economic, cultural or racial, linguistic or geographic—or a combination of several of these. A parish that offers sanctuary to a refugee family from another part of the world is not itself traveling, but its social, cultural, linguistic, and probably racial mission certainly has a geographic dimension as people seek to understand the conditions that the refugee family fled. Offering meals for the homeless in the parish hall typically builds bridges over many social, economic, cultural, and racial borders and is therefore mission. The New England youth going to Appalachia crossed all those borders, including some linguistic differences they did not expect! Traveling to another country to teach, evangelize, or build houses is certainly a way of engaging those different from ourselves, so global mission is an important expression of the mission impulse.

∼ _What do we really mean by the word "mission"?_
It is helpful, first, to have a definition that applies to all religious mission, so that we can understand what Christian mission shares with today's strong mission impulses in such religions as Islam, Buddhism, and Hinduism. _Religious mission consists of the spiritual vision and the practical means through which people project their religious faith and work and invite the participation and adherence of others._ This definition applies

equally to Anglican Frontier Missions, the Chicago Islamic Center, the New Earth and Blessed Peace Buddhist Meditation Society up the street from where I live, the Bahai Foi Centre d'Information in Montreal, and the Hare Krishna Temple in Newcastle-upon-Tyne. All of these groups have a spiritual vision, and in one way or another they are promoting their faith and inviting others to participate in their way of life.

It is helpful, second, to define *Christian mission* concisely in a way that distinguishes it from the mission of other religions and from other kinds of Christian work. *Christian mission is the activity of sending and being sent across significant boundaries of human experience to bear witness in word and deed to God's action in Christ in the power of the Holy Spirit.* Mission means sending and being sent, and it involves moving beyond who and where we are to encounter situations, people, and cultures that challenge and extend our experience. This is as true of a Korean Presbyterian missionary to Japan as it is of a Church of South India missionary to Assam, in India's northeast, or of a South American Missionary Society church planter from Georgia starting new congregations in Chile. Witness to the activity of the triune God in word and deed defines the content of Christian mission in a way that includes the full breadth of mission work: evangelism and social justice, medicine and education, reconciliation and simple presence.

～ *What basis can there be for getting involved in other places, especially sending missionaries to other countries, when there is so much to be done in our own backyard?* Housing activists in North America often run up against what they call the NIMBY syndrome (NIMBY is the acronym for Not In My Back Yard). People in affluent communities may favor affordable housing in the abstract, but "NIMBY!" is the response when an actual project is proposed close to home. The second mission question is the opposite of NIMBY: "Why go elsewhere when there's so much to do right here IMBY?!" Our comprehensive understanding of mission helps us realize that mission frontiers are not only in other countries. Reaching out to people down the street may be more urgent and more difficult than engaging needs in other societies and nations. In addition, we are wary of being blind and arrogant in presuming that we can help solve problems abroad when we have so many that we have not solved at home: racism and bigotry of many kinds, youth violence, widening gaps between rich and poor, and a widespread agnosticism that calls the church to reframe its message to young adults. Why send teachers to Honduras when public schools are decaying in our own inner cities? What do we have to offer to racial tensions in the new South Africa when racial conflicts are smoldering in Liverpool, Toronto, and Los Angeles? Why send a pastor to strengthen evangelism in Japan when Anglican witness seems to be declining in the United Kingdom, Canada, and the United States?

Here are two initial reflections to ponder in response to this important question. First, as the new millennium opens we are ever more aware that we live in a global village where interdependence and intercommunication, not isolation, are the keynotes. What happens in one community affects all other communities, and most regional issues are shared by people in other societies as well. Loyalties and obligations can no longer be purely local, and increasingly we see the importance of being global citizens. Indeed, the ethnocentric paroxysms of the Balkans and

Rwanda illustrate the dangers of allowing one's local identity to define and limit the breadth of one's empathy and engagement. We may feel we face a dilemma between the local and the global, but, again, the choice is not *either–or* but *both–and.* "Think globally, act locally," says a popular bumper sticker, to which we might add, "The global is local, so think and act both!"

Second, solving problems is not the primary motive of Christian mission. Historically, the western mission enterprise has worked intensively in education, healthcare, agriculture, and technical training, but those contributions have been the fruit of a foundational vision of building community around the gospel, simply being with people in the presence of Christ. Responding to human need expresses the fullness of the gospel and is inherent in Christian mission, but sheer solidarity in suffering may be the most helpful starting place in that response. From such a vantage point, we realize we have as much to learn from others as we have to give. We become more open to working as partners with the people we seek to help, and we see more clearly the shortcomings of our own societies. Fixing things, solving problems, and resolving conflicts are common western approaches to the Two-Thirds World, and they have tended to create as many problems as they have solved, whether through the churches, governmental agencies, or private voluntary organizations.

~ *With all that the twentieth century realized about the mistakes of western mission in other cultures, isn't it important that western churches avoid meddling in other cultures in the twenty-first century?*

This is the question asked most frequently about Christian global mission. Mistakes that Christian mis-

sionaries from the Global North made in their work in
the Global South have become so well known that
caution and suspicion are the first reactions many
people have to the mention of world mission. Many
missionaries have dismissed the primal religions of
Africa and Polynesia and have demonized such world
religions as Hinduism, Buddhism, and Islam. Some
have presented the gospel through their own ethnic
and cultural identity, depicting Jesus, for instance, as
a blonde European. Missionaries have sometimes not
bothered to learn the language of the people to whom
they were sent, insisting that their hosts should learn
English or French or German. Some missionaries have
disparaged and dismissed indigenous cultures as lack-
ing worthwhile values and have sought to substitute
western norms. In their evangelistic zeal, they have
ignored human needs, and some have lived a lifestyle
far removed from that of the people they seek to
serve. The style and content of development projects
have sometimes been misconceived and poorly implemented.

It is very important that Christians in the Global
North absorb this history and avoid naive optimism
about mission, both historically and for the future. It
is equally important that we not be paralyzed by this
history. In this book we will explore a vision for mission in the twenty-first century, but here are some
preliminary reflections to ponder. Not only is
Christianity now a global religion, but Christians in
many recently evangelized societies have vital and
growing autonomous churches, and they have their
own affirmations and critiques of the western missionary enterprise. These indigenous Christians
describe the mistakes that western missionaries made
much more acutely and eloquently than we can, for
they experience them from the inside. Often they also

celebrate how missionaries preached the gospel, established churches, and founded institutions of education and healthcare that continue to be crucial in the indigenous churches' witness in newly independent nations. Assessments by those on the receiving end, in other words, tend to be more balanced between shortcomings and gifts, while our own soul-searching is often more uniformly negative about the past and pessimistic about the future. If we are serious about learning from our partners, we need to listen to their perspective on the missionary legacy. In this book, chapter three reviews general mission history, while chapter four explores the Anglican and Episcopal mission story.

The critique of mistakes points toward an ideal of missionary attitude and work that far exceeds the standards expected of diplomats or multinational corporate executives, whose global reach now rivals that of the western mission enterprise. The higher standard is appropriate, for religious mission deals with the totality of life. The very passion of the mission critique testifies to the fact that people continue to harbor an ideal of what mission should look like and how a Christian missionary should work. Even as we ask incredulously, "How could missionaries *do* that?!" we seem to be saying, "*This* is how it should be done!"—which assumes that *some* sort of mission is appropriate and that it *can* be done right. In fact, the lessons learned from missionary mistakes over the last several centuries constitute an enormous body of scholarly literature and practical lore that helps guide mission work in a new millennium. In addition, it is important to realize that mission is not exclusively an initiative of the northern or western churches. Growing numbers of missionaries are sent out by churches in such countries as Korea, India, and Kenya, and they are companions from whom we have much to learn. Chapter six in this book explores the important relationship between Christian mission and human cultures.

∼ *Other religions are rich in spirit, so why try to evangelize people who may already be religious?*
In 1929, a mission scholar named Daniel Johnson Fleming published an article in *Christian Century* entitled "If Buddhists Came to Our Town."[5] It was an arresting title at the time because so few Americans had experienced Buddhism or any religious tradition other than Christianity. Beginning in the 1960s, people in North America and western Europe experienced a quantum leap in their experience of diverse religious traditions. Now the person moving next door might very well be a Buddhist, Hindu, Muslim, Sikh, or perhaps a Bahai or Jain. One factor, of course, is immigration by people with these religious affiliations, so that most major cities in Europe and North America now have Muslim mosques, Hindu temples, and Buddhist meditation centers. Muslims in the United States now outnumber Episcopalians, a situation that could scarcely have been foreseen in 1929![6] In addition, in coming to "our town," groups within major world religions have undertaken various kinds of mission that have resulted in many North Americans and Europeans adopting these religious faiths. The result is that the countries of Europe and North America are now much more diverse in their religious makeup than they were fifty years ago.

In this religious variety, many Christians in the West have come to respect the spirituality and personal integrity of their neighbors and co-workers who embrace other religions, whether they are immigrants, descendants of recent immigrants, or native-born converts to another faith. The traditions of so-called primal religions, such as those of Africans or American Indians, are now taken more seriously. All this raises theological questions. "I experience spiritual fulfillment in Christ," a western Christian might ask, "but does that mean everyone else must? How can Christ be the only way, if so many people worldwide experience God through other religious traditions? Isn't dialogue rather than competition the best route for relations among the religions? If the real mission field is the absence of any religious faith, shouldn't the religions join forces to address secularism? And shouldn't we join forces to combat poverty, racism, and injustice of all kinds? If so, what place is there for Christian mission to people of other faiths?" These interreligious questions are addressed specifically in chapter five, but they form an important background for every exploration of mission.

～ *Since Christianity seems to be growing elsewhere, especially in Africa and Latin America, what do western Christians have to offer as missionaries?*
During the twentieth century Christianity saw phenomenal growth in the Two-Thirds World, so called because it contains two-thirds of the world's population. In 1900, 34.5 percent of the world's 1.6 billion people were Christian, and 82 percent of these lived in Europe and North America, with 11 percent in Latin America. At the turn of the twenty-first century, 33 percent of the world's 6 billion people are Christians, so the Christian proportion has decreased slightly. Now, however, Europe and North America account for just 41 percent of the Christians, while Africa has 18 percent, Asia 16 percent, and Latin America 24 per-

cent. In Africa, the number of Christians increased over thirtyfold during the twentieth century, from 10 to 360 million, constituting a fivefold increase in the percentage represented by Christians there, from 9 to 46 percent. Worldwide, Anglicans in Africa, Asia, and Latin America now outnumber Anglicans in Europe, North America, and Oceania, 44 million to 36 million.[7] Numbers tell only part of the story, for Christians in other parts of the world have developed enormous spiritual vitality and dynamic forms of church life that have much to offer to the global church. Given these Christian and Anglican demographics, why should Anglican missionaries continue to be sent from Europe and North America? With Christianity declining in many western countries, shouldn't the Global South send missionaries to the Global North?

Missionaries are indeed being sent now from the Two-Thirds World to Europe and North America, and Anglican visitors from Asia, Africa, and Latin America have revived the spirituality of many in our congregations. This mutual exchange of missionaries is long overdue, and represents what the World Council of Churches has called "mission in six continents." Yet partner churches in the Anglican Communion and other communions, such as the Lutheran World Federation, continue to request missionaries from Europe and North America, for they seek specially skilled people who are available from those churches—administrators, seminary instructors, church developers, media specialists, physicians, school teachers, and the like. For us, sending missionaries expresses our wider concern. It opens us to encountering others and enacts the global oneness of the church. As missionaries are themselves transformed by the gospel insights and spiritual vitality they experience in other parts of the world, they become channels of learning and inspiration for the sending churches when they return. In addition, 1.7 billion people live in parts of the world where gospel witness has been nonexistent or minimal, such as Central Asia, and there are Anglican and other mission groups specially concerned with sending missionaries to such underevangelized areas.

Broadly, Christian mission addresses fundamental questions about our identity, purpose, and function, and it includes all that God sends us to be and to do. More narrowly, it responds to God's call that we move beyond who we are and where we are to encounter the other, crossing frontiers of whatever kind to share a life in Christ. This sharing takes many different forms, depending on needs and gifts, but they all contribute to building community around the gospel. Historical developments have prompted important questions about global mission, to which this chapter has responded in a preliminary way. A fundamental reality about Christian mission, however, is that it belongs to God, not to us. What scripture reveals is that the real missionary is not the church but God, and it is to that theme that we now turn.

Chapter Two

The Missionary God in Scripture

It was night. I was sitting on the ground in a forest in eastern Zimbabwe as a preacher held forth to a crowd of Christians gathered for a dusk-to-dawn vigil of preaching, singing, praying, and, remarkably, walking on the huge fire that we were sitting around. Beside the preacher stood a reader who held a gas lantern in one hand and in the other a Shona Bible. Bending his head close to the page by the light of the lamp, the reader read out a verse, and the preacher preached it. The reader read out another verse, the preacher preached on that verse, and so on. Women and girls sat on one side of the fire, men and boys on the other. Everyone was very attentive.

The preacher's text was the last section of Mark's gospel, where Jesus addresses his disciples after rising from the dead:

And he said to them, "Go into all the world and proclaim the good news to the whole creation. The one who believes and is baptized will be saved; but the one who does not believe will be condemned." (Mark 16:15-16)

Said the preacher: "That refers to when you ministers go and travel over all lands, when you arrive and when you preach these words. A person who does not believe in these words will be judged. So the problem we have in being in the bush like this is to spread the words so that all people, when the world comes to an end, will have heard that God's words are there. There should not be anyone who would say, 'I did not hear them.'" He went on to reflect on how the world will end in fire, a prominent theme for these Christians, who walk on real fires as a way of testing the Holy Spirit's presence with them as they prepare for the end-time.

"Being in the bush like this" has never really been an obstacle to evangelism and mission for this group, called the African Apostolic Church of Johane Marange. In 1932, the young Johane Marange, a laborer in eastern Zimbabwe, saw light falling around him and heard a voice saying, "You are John the Baptist, an Apostle. Now go and do my work! Go to every country and preach and convert people!" Marange and his followers did just that. Since then, the Apostles have become the second largest church in Zimbabwe, with about a million members. Crossing ethnic, linguistic, and national boundaries, they now have congregations in Mozambique, South Africa, Zambia, and Congo.

So the Bible is a touchstone for Christian mission, not just in the past, but also in the present; not only among historically mission-minded churches in the Global North, but also among newer churches in the Global South. As Christians experience God in Christ in the power of the Holy Spirit, a mission impulse to share that life with others and to invite their participation is apparently a natural fruit of that experience. At the same time, the mission impulse is informed, confirmed, and inspired by what they read in their sacred text, the Bible, believed by so many Christians to communicate the word of God in the life of the human family. Thus the night-time preacher turned to scripture to reflect on the mission work of the Marange Apostles. There he found direction and authority for the mission to which he believed God was calling the faithful. He focused on Mark's version of what, in Matthew's gospel, has come to be known as the Great Commission, understood by many Christians the world over as Jesus' command to proclaim the gospel to all peoples.

The Marange Apostles are a distinctive church, for they walk on fire, avoid pork and alcohol, and embrace polygamy, the practice of one man having several wives—all on the basis of scripture. I interpret the Bible differently on these and other points, so my theology differs from the Apostles'. As a result, the Apostles do not accept me fully as a fellow Christian. Once, for instance, a group of Apostles who knew me to be an Anglican priest urged me to seek baptism at their hands, so that I could be saved and be their missionary in North America. Regardless of how they view me, however, I bear witness to the authenticity and vitality of their faith in Christ, and I honor their commitment to mission. Christians can disagree in their interpretation of the Bible but still have a unique and powerful unity, both in the Holy Spirit and, oddly enough, in the fact that we all look to the same Bible for guidance in the midst of our disagreements about how we should interpret it.

This chapter explores the theme of mission in scripture. It highlights how the impetus of Christian mission is rooted in God's relationship with the human community as presented by scripture. Among Anglicans there is a wide range of views about how to interpret scripture, from conservative and evangelical to liberal and postmodern, from a view that the Bible is the infallible utterance *of* God to a view that it is the fallible reflections of people *about* God. The Episcopal Catechism offers a centrist view of scripture that represents the views of most Anglicans. In response to the question, "Why do we call the Holy Scriptures the Word of God?" it answers, "We call them the Word of God because God inspired their human authors and because God still speaks to us through the Bible" (BCP 853). With that understanding we hear scripture readings acclaimed in the liturgy as "The Word of the Lord," to which we respond, "Thanks be to God." For our reflection on mission, scripture offers foundational insights about the God we worship, the direction of God's movement in the human story, and the history of how people have responded to God's presence in their lives.

God is the missionary at the heart of Christian mission—that is a central insight of scripture. Although the Catechism talks about the mission of the church, our starting place needs to be the mission of God. Mission is not fundamentally something we do as Christians but a quality of God's own being. It is not a program of ours but the path of God's action in the world. The mission of the church, therefore, derives from the mission of God, and it has meaning only in relation to what God is up to in the universe. Already engaged in mission, God simply invites us to participate in what God is doing.

As we travel with the missionary God in this chapter, we begin with the creation stories. We then consider the call of Abraham, the ministry of Jesus, and the outreach of the early church. We end with the vision found in the Revelation to St. John the Divine of all peoples gathered around the glory of God at the consummation of all things.

∾ God's Mission in Creation

The creation accounts in the first two chapters of Genesis offer truth about God through stories, and they present a picture of God on a mission. "In the beginning when God. . . "—when God *what?*—God *did* something: "God *created* the heavens and the earth." Not "God contemplated, or considered, or reflected," but "God *created.*" The first thing predicated of God in scripture is not a quality or an attribute or a person- ality trait, but an active verb that requires a direct object. God is the God who acts. Genesis presents God's action as bringing forth existence out of non- existence; being out of potential being; specific, differ- entiated, and fulfilled kinds of life out of the chaos that was "a formless void." And how does God do that? In the first Genesis story, God does no more than speak and things come to be. The sheer word of God fuses plan and implementation, vision and fulfillment, in one perfect act of creation. None of what we learn about God here conflicts with the findings of geology and paleontology or with theories of evolution, for the story seeks to communicate the nature or the inner meaning of God, of the universe, and of humanity.

So God the creator is an enterprising, activist God, busy on an errand—all marks of being on a mission. But what is the intent and meaning of that mission? What can we infer from the creation accounts about *why* God created the universe? I suggest that God's central intention was to create *a community of life*. Community needed an environment of glory in sky and earth, mountain and sea. Community was consti- tuted of life abundant in both quantity and variety, in the midst of which humanity was to have a pivotal place: "Let us make humankind in our image, according to our likeness" (1:26). In the second creation story the human was formed from the humus (2:7), and this very earthy creature bears the image of the God who, in the words of a familiar hymn, "dwells in light inaccessible, hid from our eyes." What does it mean to be created in the image of God? It means, the Catechism tells us, "that we are free to make choices: to love, to create, to reason, and to live in harmony with creation and with God" (BCP 845). God, who is life itself, reached out and created a living being who bears the very imprint of all that is central in God, and who also has the capacity to turn away from God and do all that is contrary to who God is and what God envisions for the universe.

This drama suggests that longing is a central personality trait in God. That may surprise us, for we are used to thinking of God as all-sufficient, and longing implies needing or wanting something beyond oneself or something that does not yet exist. Yes, indeed, God felt the need for company beyond God, beyond even the trinitarian community within God. God did want something that did not yet exist. God yearned for a mutual relationship with other beings, mutual in that God could both give and receive. The mission that God expressed in creation was to give birth to a community of life where there could be just such mutuality and growth. For the community to be authentic, God needed to give up control. Willing to do that, God created beings who are truly free, all for the sake of community that would be not nominal or false, but full and genuine. God's creative work was mission because in creation God moved out on an errand, and the errand was to share God's life. So God brought into being life which not only was distinguishable from

God but which also had the capacity to separate itself from God. God was the first missionary.

This way of looking at God delivers us from a long-standing Christian tendency to see mission exclusively as fixing what is broken. In the church we have developed many different understandings of what the right emphasis in mission should be. Some see it primarily as the evangelism of preaching the gospel to those who have not heard it, while others focus on relief and development work, as in bringing supplies to the flood-stricken, food to the hungry, hospitals to the sick, or classrooms to the unschooled. Still others highlight liberation for the captives, justice for the oppressed, and power for the powerless. All these approaches share a basic assumption that mission means responding to the needs of people who lack something, addressing deficiencies and distortions in human situations, repairing the torn fabric of people's lives and communities. That is indeed an important thrust of mission, since the course of the world has scarcely been what God intended in creation—which is why the Catechism says the mission of the church is to *restore* people to unity with God and one another in Christ. The unity envisioned by God was fractured, so mission often focuses on restoration, on fixing what is broken.

If God was on a mission in creation, however, it means that fixing what is broken does not exhaust the content of mission, for in the beginning there was nothing to fix. Instead, God acted with a longing for relationship, and God's mission brought into being a community of life. Since mission began not at the moment of human sin and alienation but at the moment of creation, we can see that for us as well mission consists most fundamentally in reaching out to form relationships in which we experience a community of life. In the present state of the world, after the so-called fall of humanity, it seems that there is always something to fix. Fixing is secondary, however, to simply forming relationships and nourishing community.

～ Calling One to Reach Many

As human beings exercised their freedom to oppose God's designs, the drama of the created world did not work out as God had hoped. Pride and rebellion dispelled harmony of will between God and humanity, and alienation distorted the community of life for which the universe was created. Discord, injustice, and violence afflicted the ancient world and continue to torment our own.

In this environment God longed to restore harmony with the human family, yearned for reconciliation. Out of that longing came God's remarkable call to Abraham: "Go from your country and your kindred and your father's house to the land that I will show you. I will make of you a great nation . . . and in you all the families of the earth shall be blessed" (Genesis 12:1-3). Extraordinary! Out of the anguish that God experienced in the pain, grief, and discord of all humanity, God cried out to one, solitary human being. With Abraham, God narrowed down to the microcosm of one person's response, one person's faithfulness, one person's willingness to live out a covenant. God set out on a mission of reconciliation but devolved that mission on one person and his family, undertaking to work through them and to let the mission be shaped by the choices they would make.

Humility and trust mark God's initiative with Abraham. Instead of operating as an omnipotent instant fix-it-all, God gave over and entrusted the mission to a frail human being who could be counted on to make mistakes. Seeking to restore the created community of being, God stayed confident that the divine image in humanity, never entirely effaced, would draw at least one person and one family back into a faithful covenant. This reading of the story may differ from what we are used to hearing, for we often focus on the magnitude of the call and the honor that was Abraham's in receiving it. Greater still was God's humility in calling Abraham. Such trust calls the church to evaluate its outreach relationships, for missionaries and the church as a whole have sometimes found it difficult to give over the mission—especially its money and its institutions!—to those to whom the gospel has been proclaimed. Surely, if God could entrust all to Abraham—and to us—we should be able to entrust one another with the mission we have received.

The call to Abraham establishes the remarkably consistent biblical theme of God choosing one to reach many. Abraham was chosen not primarily for his own benefit but for the benefit of many. God planned to do something special with him, and through that work, however it might turn out, "all the families of the earth shall be blessed." In a story that can seem microcosmic and parochial—the rest of Genesis does nothing more than chronicle the stumblings and minor triumphs of the first four generations—it turns out that the vision of Abraham's call was global from the outset. Through Abraham God was embarking on a cosmic reconstruction, for through his clan the love and faithfulness of God were to reconcile and transform the whole human family.

The call to Abraham represented a choice on God's part. From that choice grew the people of Israel, whom the Bible often calls God's "chosen people." That concept prompts concern about mission today

when we consider how the religious notion of "chosenness" has been used to oppress others. Palestinian
Christians and Muslims, for instance, feel dispossessed
when some Israeli Jews insist that a particular set of
geographic borders has divine sanction in the Torah.
Roman Catholic *conquistadors* in Central America and
the Philippines used a belief in divine chosenness to
justify killing entire peoples, as in Hispaniola, and the
enslavement of others. A sense of manifest destiny
prompted Protestant settlers to wage continual war-
fare against the original inhabitants of North
America. Apartheid in South Africa was buttressed by
Afrikaners' conviction that God had chosen them for
that land. All of us have experienced how the sense of
being "in God's will" can prompt people to disparage
others and to create exclusive clubs of the chosen.

This was certainly true in Jesus' day as well.
Scandalized by priestly corruption in the Jerusalem
temple, the Pharisees were leading a lay renewal
movement to restore true devotion to Judaism. It was
clear to Jesus, though, that their zeal had turned pernicious, for self-righteousness took them further from
God than the people they sought to purify. Yet Jesus
himself felt specially chosen as he heard God say at his
baptism, "You are my beloved son," and this sustained
him as a missionary throughout Judea and Galilee.

Being chosen by God is an experience and a conviction that becomes distorted when we succumb to our
insecurity, pride, and ambition. Indeed, that is the
story of much of the Old Testament as God's people
turned their chosenness into a refuge of complacency
and a tool for oppressing immigrants, the poor, and
political adversaries. In response, God turned repeatedly back to one person—Moses, Deborah, Hannah,
Samuel, David, Nathan, and all the prophets—as a
way of trying yet again to reach the unfaithful many.

It is from Isaiah that we have the Epiphany versicle reminding Israel that its mission was outward and global, not inward and parochial: "I will give you as a light to the nations, that my salvation may reach to the end of the earth" (Isaiah 49:6b). Thus, distortion of the mission principle of choosing one to reach many prompted repeated renewals: over and over God remedied distortions among the many by reverting to one.

The missionary nature of the church is likewise a case of one being chosen to reach many. Regarded as a single entity, the church is such a one chosen to reach many, a single mustard seed planted in the great and tangled weedfield of the world. Many enterprises in the church's world mission are instances of one being chosen to reach many. The vision for canceling the debts of poor countries through Jubilee 2000, for instance, was received by a few people on different continents, and their dogged faithfulness transformed an apparent pipedream into a worldwide movement. The work of Mother Teresa's Missionaries of Charity began with one Albanian nun looking into the eyes of one dying man in Calcutta and seeing there the face of Jesus. As the best-known missionary of the twentieth century, more widely known than Albert Schweitzer was in an earlier day, Teresa's witness reached countless millions. Practically every missionary who feels called by God wonders, "I am just one. What am I among so many? Is this practical? Is this just my pride?" The reality is that the missionary God works *through* individuals, choosing so often a *one*, with all the frailty of that *one*, in order to reach many.

∾ God's Mission Incarnate in Jesus
"And the Word became flesh and lived among us ... " (John 1:14). So also the mission of God became flesh

and lived among us in Jesus of Nazareth. The mission
that God spoke in the act of creation, the mission that
the longing God pursued through the callings and
alienations and reconciliations of Israel's saga—all
this vision and struggle took flesh in the biography of
one human being. Enfleshment, after all, is what the
word "incarnation" means. Jesus compels our faith
and our mission vision through the self-emptying of
God by which we can say both "In Jesus we see God"
and "In Jesus we see what it means to be human." In
taking flesh, God emptied God's self of the divine
attributes of omnipotence, omnipresence, and, most
important, omniscience. Jesus had to come by his
vision of God and his sense of mission the way we
do—by listening, growing in a tradition, praying,
sorting truth from distortion, struggling with temp-
tations. Again, God turned to one in order to reach
many. In *this* one, God humbly took the risk that the
very character and integrity of God could be altered
through the decisions of this one person, in whom the
very being of God was incarnate. In short, Jesus could
have failed—but he did not. The longing God's ultimate risk was answered by the longing Jesus' ultimate faithfulness. No wonder that luminous embrace
defines our sense of who God is, what we are meant
to be as human beings, and what our mission is in the
world!

God's act of becoming incarnate must be central in
any understanding of Christian mission. This is especially true for Anglicans, who take the incarnation as
a theological starting-place. As always, words and
visions were available to God, but, finally, becoming
one *with* us by becoming one *of* us was the only way
forward. The risk of embodied presence is crucial in
mission. Anglican reserve has often nurtured an
objectivity that produces sound theology and steady

policy, excellent position papers and handsome books, but not personal engagement. Similarly, as global mission has become more complex, sending money to solve problems has sometimes seemed easier than sending people. As electronic communication blossoms, e-mail and videoconferences can seem convenient and inexpensive ways of doing mission around the world. Books, money, and electronics do help a great deal, but they are disembodied. At the heart of mission is the incarnational event of real people being with real people. As missionaries allow their own living to mesh with the living of others, they open themselves to being profoundly affected by others. Just as God's incarnation project was risky, so also encounters in world mission are risky. For all, there is the risk of being personally changed, especially as we give up privileges that we are used to. For some, there is the risk of violence and disease. God's risky self-emptying in Christ is our model for this mission journey.

Empowered by the Holy Spirit in his baptism, Jesus burst into ministry proclaiming, "The time is fulfilled, and the kingdom of God has come near" (Mark 1:15). This proclamation was foundational for Jesus' mission, and it must be for ours as well. Jesus preached a great deal about how we should live with God and with one another as he addressed prayer, ethics, and justice, but all of his teachings issued from his vision of the kingdom of God. Think of how many parables begin with the words "The kingdom of God is like . . . " or "The kingdom of heaven may be compared to. . . . " The kingdom proclamation expressed Jesus' conviction that *God was up to something!* Ever acting and activist, God was inaugurating a new way of being present and reigning in the world. Jesus was intensely aware that he himself was the catalyst for this inbreaking kingdom through all the activities of his ministry and through his very being. As he said about Isaiah's jubilee proclamation when he finished reading in the Nazareth synagogue, "Today this scripture has been fulfilled in your hearing" (Luke 4:21). What seized Jesus was a vision of God on the move in the world, and this is what he wished on his hearers. He was saying to them, "God is up to something! Open your eyes to see God at work. Open your ears to hear God calling. Discern what God is doing, then join God in that mission."

Jesus' proclamation establishes a different starting place for mission. Despite all the crying needs of the world, the first questions turn out *not* to be "What are the needs?" or "What should we do to address them?" Instead, we need to ask, "What is God up to? What new thing is God inviting us to participate in?" The mood shifts from obligation to the eager expectancy for the kingdom that pervaded Jesus' ministry. Spiritual discernment, not a to-do list for the world, becomes the first step in planning mission. Excitement replaces duty as we recognize an opportunity to participate in a drama much larger than ourselves, and we leave behind the illusion that God's mission depends on our performance. We respond to God's invitation, rather than working up an initiative on our own. Often we do not even have a full picture, but just a hint and a hunch, and God is asking us to participate in planting some mustard seed so small it seems absurd. Without exaggerating our own role, we yet know that God is using us as catalysts for the kingdom. We realize that God *needs* people who are willing to speak and act in ways that prompt others to recognize and participate in what God is up to.

Those who sense that the kingdom mission begins with a vision of God's initiative plunge into the world with a passion for healing the whole person and all of life. Jesus embraced it all. His mission was holistic as he reached out to heal body, mind, and spirit and to challenge the structural patterns of society. To the paralytic he said both, "Your sins are forgiven" and "Stand up, take your mat and go to your home" (Mark 2:5, 11). To the demons possessing a man wandering among tombs he said, "Come out of the man!" (Mark 5:8). He harangued the legal establishment: "Beware of the scribes. . . . They devour widows' houses and for the sake of appearance say long prayers" (Mark 12:38-40). The final judgment, said Jesus, will hinge on these criteria: "I was hungry and you gave me food, I was thirsty and you gave me something to drink, I was a stranger and you welcomed me, I was naked and you gave me clothing, I was sick and you took care of me, I was in prison and you visited me" (Matthew 25:35-36). Yet to busy Martha, annoyed by her sister's eagerness to sit still and listen, he said, "Mary has chosen the better part" (Luke 10:42). The kingdom of God was breaking in on every aspect of experience, and Jesus knew that it touched different people differently. For Jesus there was no basis for elevating certain kinds of mission, no room for prejudice against evangelism or social justice, against prayer or medicine. Throughout his holistic ministry Jesus had an explicit missionary consciousness of being *sent*, declaring, for instance, "My food is to do the will of him who sent me and to complete his work" (John 4:34), and, in Capernaum, "I must proclaim the good news of the kingdom of God to the other cities also; for I was sent for this purpose" (Luke 4:43).

A gracious gift in the gospels is that Jesus does not come across as the omnicompetent missionary, perfect from the start in his mission understanding and work. Like us, he learned from others. From a Syrophoenician woman asking that her demon-possessed daughter be healed we learn with him that it is often on the margins that we discover what our mission is, and from those to whom we do not feel called (Mark 7:24–30). The harshness of his retort, "It is not fair to take the children's food and throw it to the dogs," is startling, but Jesus had gone on retreat into foreign territory precisely to get away from the press of people's needs in Judea and Galilee. Desperate to be replenished with peace and quiet, he initially turned away the woman's plea that he heal her daughter. The justification he gives her suggests that, while Jesus probably always sensed that the scope of God's kingdom was universal, he initially believed that his own direct mission was limited to the Jewish people. After all, his faith tradition saw the Jews as God's "chosen people." Gentiles were dogs. Foreign territory was retreat territory, a respite from being on mission.

I hear the bystanders chuckling at the woman's plucky reply—"Sir, even the dogs under the table eat the children's crumbs"—but at a stroke Jesus' mission vision was enlarged. He realized that there was no limit to the community God wanted to reach and that the lives and needs of all people were precious to God. He did not learn this from a rabbi, but from a Gentile, someone who was thought to know nothing about God's vision. Equally remarkable, he learned this not from a man but from a woman. Although Jewish scripture abounds with tales of remarkable women— Sarah, Miriam, Hannah, Deborah, Esther, and others—Jewish religious culture in Jesus' time did not envisage a woman being able to teach a prophet like Jesus. Jesus here encountered the other, and from this other he learned something crucial about God's mission. This and other experiences planted the seed of what became the Great Commission, the command Matthew says the risen Jesus gave to his disciples, "Go therefore and make disciples of all nations" (Matthew 28:19-20). The Greek word for "nations" here—*ethne* (pronounced eth-nay, from which our English word "ethnic" comes)—is used in the New Testament specifically for Gentiles, that is, for non-Jewish people groups. Thus the Great Commission declares that the gospel is urgently important for all peoples to experience, not just one people or a few selected peoples, and that in Christ God has confirmed a new covenant that includes the entire human family.

The famous Christ-hymn in Paul's letter to the Philippians (2:6-11) suggests that becoming incarnate was a self-emptying act by Christ. The hymn goes on to stress that the particular events to which Jesus submitted in his life continued that self-emptying: "And being found in human form, he humbled himself and became obedient to the point of death—even death on a cross." Isn't it remarkable that the most commonly used image for the world's most populous religion is an instrument of torture and death? Amazingly, probably a majority of the crosses around the world—whether in China or Canada, Borneo or Bolivia—actually show the central figure of our faith in agony and dying. Whether a particular depiction or statue is a crucifix or an empty cross, it asserts that Jesus' humility in accepting the premature, unjust, and abusive termination of his life is a central drama in the relationship between God and humanity. Jesus' self-spending ministry to others climaxed in the crucifixion, a distilled example of loving service and its possible cost. Because Jesus signifies God to us, as well as faithful human living, his sacrificial love reveals what God is like: responsive to our needs, longing for reconciliation, living in solidarity, willing to serve to the point of self-eclipse.

Popular Christianity often views the missionary calling as the pinnacle of self-sacrifice, exceeding the self-sacrifice of other religious vocations such as ordained ministry and monastic life, and human service vocations such as public school teaching and social work. Why is that? It is partly because many missionaries have indeed suffered in obvious ways: disease, discomfort, persecution, and sometimes death. It may also be that many Christians realize intuitively that the calling and ministry of Christ was a missionary vocation in the sense of going out to encounter others. Although we realize increasingly that all Christians are called to be missionary in their life and work, the cross-cultural missionary recapitulates literally and vividly God's movement of going out to encounter and embrace the other, for the missionary leaves a home culture with all its familiar assumptions and exposes himself or herself to the unpredictable and sometimes threatening environment and culture of another people. Similarly, and whether rightly or wrongly, the Christian missionary is often *expected* to be more self-sacrificing than clergy or human service workers—to live on less, accept privation with equanimity, and face danger bravely. Our Friday prayer "that we, walking in the way of the cross, may find it none other than the way of life and peace" (BCP 99) is one that many Anglicans see especially fulfilled in the ideal of the missionary vocation.

What we tend not to see so clearly is that the resurrection and ascension of Jesus are also pivotal for understanding Christian mission. In the resurrection the wounded God was made whole again, catalyzed to heal the rift between God and humanity. The followers of Jesus soon became bearers of this good news. "I have seen the Lord!" exclaimed Mary Magdalene as she became the first missionary of the risen Christ

(John 20:18). "As the Father has sent me, so I send you," Jesus said to his followers after the resurrection (John 20:21). There he devolved on them his own experience of being sent by God, so that now they were just as sent as he had been, with tasks in the world comparable to his own. What we term the ascension of Jesus into heaven was simply a final resurrection appearance, designed to signal that the risen Jesus would not continue to appear here and there, and that henceforth his followers had a vital role in fulfilling the mission. As in Jesus' kingdom proclamation, that mission would be energized by the conviction that God was up to something in the world, only now that conviction was grounded and verified in the servant life, sacrificial death, and victorious resurrection of Jesus, who became integral to the mission proclamation. Relationship with the risen Christ was the door into a full and reconciled relationship with God.

∽ Mission Diffused in the Early Church

As with Jesus, the New Testament accounts of the early church are an inexhaustible mine of insight about Christian mission, but three developments stand out: mission communities empowered by the Holy Spirit, the movement of the gospel into the multicultural world of non-Jews, and gospel proclamation to the known world.

"As the Father has sent me, so I send you," said Jesus to his disciples, after which "he breathed on them and said to them, 'Receive the Holy Spirit'" (John 20:21-22). The wind from God that swept over the waters at creation, the breath that God breathed into the first human—this wind and breath Jesus now breathed into his friends and constituted them as a community of the new humanity birthed by his own death and resurrection. In Luke's narrative, the Holy Spirit arrived on the day of Pentecost with the sound of wind and a vision of tongues of flame (Acts 2:1-12). Jesus-folk cowering from the authorities and wondering what to do next were transformed into a community that proclaimed the gospel in such compelling words and mighty deeds that it grew exponentially, prompted official censure, and began multiplying communities as persecution dispersed its members into the Mediterranean world.

It was the outpouring of the Holy Spirit that created this mass movement. As the Spirit propelled Jesus into mission at his baptism, so the Spirit at Pentecost propelled Jesus' followers into mission. The Holy Spirit is the person of the trinitarian God we often have more trouble identifying, understanding, and invoking than God the Father or God the Son. The Catechism highlights the dynamic nature of the Spirit in implementing God's designs: "The Holy Spirit is the Third Person of the Trinity, God at work in the world and in the Church even now" (BCP 852). Yet this description, like the now common designation of the Spirit as "sustainer," is too mild. The Spirit is the fire that brings God's presence close, prompting the ecstasy Jesus experienced when he "rejoiced in the Holy Spirit" upon his disciples' return from their second mission trip (Luke 10:17-24). It is the Spirit who moves the depths of our souls, praying through us, as the apostle Paul says, "with sighs too deep for words" (Romans 8:26). It is the Spirit who catalyzes the restless, yearning, passionate dimension of the religious life. In all these ways and more, the Holy Spirit empowers God's people, filling them with the joy, vision, and confidence that enable them to be bold in extending God's reign in the life of the world. The specifically "pentecostal" or "charismatic" gifts of the

Spirit, such as tongues and ecstatic prophecy, are especially vivid examples of how ordinary Christians are empowered by the Spirit. With whatever gifts one has received—and Paul emphasizes to the Corinthians wisdom, knowledge, faith, healing, and administration alongside prophecy and tongues (1 Corinthians 12)—the Spirit draws us into the flow of God's mission. Mission is not a task supported by an abstract theory, but a personal outreach of God through the Holy Spirit, who invites and empowers God's people to participate in that outreach.

The letters of Paul testify to the most important and remarkable event in the life of the Jesus movement, the transformation from being a sect of Judaism in Judea and Galilee to being a cross-cultural movement reaching out to Gentiles beyond Palestine as well as to Jews. The roots of Jesus and his gospel were Jewish, and we have seen how the incarnation of God in Jesus was the culmination of God's mission impulse to reach the many of the world through one particular people, Israel. Jesus' first followers were Jewish, and their first audiences, around the year 33, were Jerusalem Jews in street, temple, and home. Yet soon after the year 40, the apostle Paul, himself a Jew, was writing to a well-established Christian community in Thessalonica, and other letters have survived from the next fifteen years to the "saints" in Corinth, Rome, and Philippi. These were important Greek and Roman cities, and the letters indicate that the recipients were mostly Gentiles, as well as Jewish Christians. Paul's letter to the Galatians stresses to an exclusively Gentile audience of Christians that the Galatian Christians did not have to become Jewish through circumcision in order to be authentically Christian. The issue was extremely controversial (Galatians 1-2; Acts 15), and one can under-

stand the Jewish Christian point of view: why should-
n't Gentile believers honor God's history with Israel
and Jesus' Jewish self-understanding by being cir-
cumcised as "proselytes," the traditional way of
Gentiles joining God's covenant with Israel?

The insight of Paul and other early leaders who
proclaimed the gospel freely to Gentiles was that in
Christ God was doing a new thing with the covenant
with Israel. God was extending it, as originally intended, to all peoples, and entry was now through faith
rather than through submission to the law given
through Moses. With the Galatian and Roman
Christians, Paul argues that all this was implicit in
God's covenant with Abraham, who was accepted not
through the law, which did not yet exist, but through
faith, and through such faith God's promise to bless
all nations was now being fulfilled (Galatians 3:6-9;
Romans 4). The relationship between faith and works
in our life with God is familiar today as an issue of
theology and spirituality, but for Paul and others in
the early Christian movement it was a crucial mission
question. If Gentile believers were going to be required
to become Jewish before they could become Christian,
the movement could stagnate quickly. Although non-
Jews attended the synagogues found in practically
every city of the Roman world, relatively few took the
major physical and social step of becoming Jewish
proselytes. Paul argues that all ethnic, gender, and
power relations are erased in Christ as all become
equally heirs of Abraham:

> . . . for in Christ Jesus you are all children of God
> through faith. As many of you as were baptized
> into Christ have clothed yourselves with Christ.
> There is no longer Jew or Greek, there is no
> longer slave or free, there is no longer male and

female; for all of you are one in Christ Jesus.
And if you belong to Christ, then you are
Abraham's offspring, heirs according to the
promise. (Galatians 3:26-29)

This declaration of full inclusion was fundamentally a
mission declaration that the gospel could and must be
offered to all, without distinction. It was the ascen-
dancy of this viewpoint that freed and energized the
gospel of Jesus to spread throughout the first-century world and, indeed, to continue its global outreach
to the present day, when that gospel has in some way
touched you and me.

Geographic diffusion is a third striking feature of
cross-cultural mission in the New Testament. The
direction shifted dramatically from centripetal mission in the Old Testament to centrifugal mission in the
New.[1] Israel was to fulfill its mission in the world by
being the light to which the rest of the world would
come—"Nations shall come to your light, and kings to
the brightness of your dawn" (Isaiah 60:3), a prophecy fulfilled in the story of the magi coming to Jesus
(Matthew 2:1-12). Israel's call was to be faithful, and
the world's call was to see the light and come to Zion
to worship, enacting a centripetal motion from the
outside in toward the center. The trajectory of early
Christianity was decidedly opposite, moving centrifugally from the center out toward the periphery, like a
stone slung from a sling. Christians understood this
outward movement to be God's mandate, as when
Paul recounted his mission call to a hostile crowd in
Jerusalem: "Then the Lord said to me, 'Go, for I will
send you far away to the Gentiles'" (Acts 22:21). The
Greek New Testament's verb for sending is *apostello*,
from which comes our word "apostle," and such apostolic sending is the distinctive mark of Christian mis-

sion, as we saw in chapter one. The centrifugal motion of going out takes us to encounter the other, and because the encounter occurs on the other's ground, we and our message become much more open to being changed by others than when they must come to us.

The modes of the gospel's centrifugal diffusion in the early church were manifold. Many Christians have inherited an impression that Christianity in its earliest days spread mainly through the labors of full-time missionaries, indefatigable travelers who constantly braved terrifying dangers in order to implement a grand design to preach the gospel to people who had never heard it. The reality of first-century mission was more complex. The witness that Jesus' followers made about him in Jerusalem was verbally eloquent, publicly miraculous, socio-economically radical, and politically defiant, but it was persecution that drove them to begin fulfilling Jesus' prediction that they would be his witnesses beyond Jerusalem— "in all Judea and Samaria, and to the ends of the earth" (Acts 1:8). The "severe persecution" that broke out against the Jerusalem church scattered believers throughout Judea and Samaria, Luke says, and "those who were scattered went from place to place, proclaiming the word" (Acts 8:1, 4). Here we meet again the call to all Christians to be missionaries in some way, for these people who preached wherever they went were not full-time, professional missionaries but ordinary believers who were suddenly refugees looking for places to live and work. They were so on fire with the gospel that they shared it in the midst of the very trauma that it had brought upon them.

Persecution was also responsible, Luke tells us, for unnamed believers taking the gospel to regions beyond Palestine—Phoenicia (today's Lebanon), the island of Cyprus, and Antioch, then a major city in what is now Turkey, where they preached to non-Jews as well as Jews. Again, this was probably in the midst of renting apartments, interviewing for jobs, arranging instruction for their children, and generally trying to keep body and soul together. Not surprisingly, it was in the non-Jewish environment of Antioch that the followers of Jesus were first called Christians, a name that emphasized the growing separation between Judaism and the Jesus movement (Acts 11:19-26). Maybe the moniker was given to the community by random Antiochenes to refer to the people, whether Jews or Gentiles, who talked about Christ. Alternatively, Gentile converts swelling the community may not have been comfortable identifying themselves as Jews, and the community needed a distinctive name. In a dynamic repeated throughout Christian history, the gospel's mission encounter with a different environment was already working changes in the self-understanding of the movement's members and on the public's perception of them.

Paul, often thought to personify the missionary stereotype, actually illustrates the diverse modes of missionary work. Paul certainly believed that God in Christ had commissioned him to proclaim the gospel, with special emphasis on "the nations." The average citizen of Corinth or Ephesus, however, probably did not see Paul as a "full-time missionary" but as one of thousands of artisans who traveled around the Mediterranean world, setting up shop in this town or the next and plying their trade. Paul spent eighteen months in Corinth primarily because he fell in with Priscilla and Aquila, who shared his tentmaking trade and who probably let him use their workshop (Acts 18:1-11). The three years he spent in Ephesus may have been occasioned by the fact that these good friends had moved there, and their still later move back to Rome perhaps encouraged Paul's plan to visit the empire's capital. Paul spent a good deal of time at his livelihood, a fact he used to remind the Thessalonians that he had not been a sponge (1 Thessalonians 2:9). The same could be said of other traveling leaders like Barnabas, Apollos, Priscilla, Aquila, Silas, Timothy, and Titus.

The book of Acts is full of conflicts between gospel emissaries and their opponents, and Paul—never one to be shy!—provides the Corinthians with an impressive catalogue of his sufferings (2 Corinthians 11:16-33), but persecution was episodic, not unremitting. While evangelism was always important, Paul's itinerary was also determined by his desire to care for churches with which he felt a special relationship. Longings (Philippians 2:19-24; Philemon 22), plans (1 Corinthians 16:5-9; Romans 15:23-29), and even threats (2 Corinthians 13:1-10) to visit congregations recur in his letters, and the book of Acts testifies to a pattern of revisiting churches (14:21-28; 20:1-38). Thus the strengthening of Christian communities walked hand-in-hand with evangelism in the missionary task, as it still does today. Paul and his companions did not work according to a grand strategy but improvised along the way as they responded to particular needs, opportunities, and obstacles. Later in his life, Paul explained his plan to visit Rome and Spain by his having proclaimed the gospel "from Jerusalem and as far around as Illyricum" in northern Greece (Romans 15:17-22), but this was a retrospective view of what he had done in the eastern Mediterranean, not an overall plan with which he started out.

In sum, the New Testament depicts the early church's explosive mission as a personal outreach of God catalyzed by the Holy Spirit. The gospel moved centrifugally outward from Palestine into the Mediterranean world through diverse impulses that included persecution, the migrations of ordinary Christians who proclaimed Christ freely wherever they went, and the efforts of leaders who sought to carry out a special missionary mandate. Most remarkably, a faith born within Judaism became a cross-cultural movement by erasing, in principle at least, all ethnic, gender, and power distinctions. It insisted that through the life, death, and resurrection of Christ the one God's ancient covenant with Abraham was now renewed and accessible to all humanity.

~ Heaven's Horizon of Mission

"When I look around this parish and see black and white and brown, and people from Europe, Africa, Asia, and South America, I like to think that this is what heaven will be like!" So said Tony Coleman, a member of St. Peter's in Cambridge. "We have lessons read in Spanish, Creole, and Yoruba," he continued. "It's a rainbow community, and that's how the church should be."

Multicultural community does glow as a salvific hope for many, as we experience the irony of over-whelming abundance growing alongside horrifying poverty after the most war-torn century of global history. We have celebrated the United Nations' first fifty years, but that coalition could not prevent genocide in Cambodia and Rwanda, nor today's ethnic and religious hatreds. Smallpox has been eradicated, but the AIDS pandemic is destroying millions in Africa and Asia. Electronic communications are ubiquitous from Lagos to São Paulo, but literacy is declining in Pakistan and Haiti. In this environment, the rush of joy that Tony feels in a parish community where all do blossom seems a harbinger of the kingdom of God that Jesus proclaimed and a foretaste of heaven.

A multicultural heaven is indeed the horizon of mission that we find in the Revelation to St. John the Divine, the last document in the New Testament and the Bible. Startling in its imagery of beasts, fiery bowls, and global cataclysms, the book of Revelation may not top your list of bedtime reading, but it is helpful to understand that it was written as resistance literature for the persecuted. It was meant to encourage Christian communities experiencing such savage attacks under the Roman emperor Domitian in the 90s of the first century that their faith and hope were languishing. In the anguish of such suffering and fear, John received visions of cosmic conflict and divine victory that bore this message: "Things look hopeless both for you and for the cause of Christ in the world, but take heart! In the cosmic struggle between God and the forces of evil, God will gain the final victory as evil is vanquished and the universe is reconciled. Moreover, know that God has already won the crucial battle in the life, death, and resurrection of Jesus, who is both the Lamb that was slain and the Lord of all lords!"

John offered visions of glory to nourish his readers' confidence in the future, and it is striking that these were multicultural visions. After the opening of the sixth seal, John testifies:

> I looked, and there was a great multitude that no one could count, from every nation, from all tribes and peoples and languages, standing before the throne and before the Lamb, robed in white, with palm branches in their hands. They cried out in a loud voice, saying, "Salvation belongs to our God who is seated on the throne,

and to the Lamb!" (Revelation 7:9-10; see also 5:6-10)

The juxtaposition of this vista with the sealing of 144,000 people from the tribes of Israel echoes the confidence we heard from Paul that the gospel's universal proclamation plays out the internal logic of God's covenant with Abraham. The consummation of all things in heaven evidently does not abolish ethnic, racial, and linguistic differences, for the heavenly crowd was not homogeneous. Instead, all the known ethnic groups were there, in their many languages, skin colors, and distinctive identities, reconciled in Christ and able to sing together a new song. The gospel's proclamation throughout the world brings the whole human family into reconciled relationship with God and with one another. This is the end-time horizon of mission with which scripture ends.

Twenty centuries later, is this not still an inviting and glorious horizon for Christian mission? Despite having long had these visions embedded within our scripture, the Christian community today is only beginning to discern and reject the racism and ethnocentrism that have afflicted our life and mission over the last many centuries. We began this chapter with the Marange Apostles looking toward the end of the world, and I noted that they hoped I would be their missionary in North America. Well, in a sense I have become that as I share the good news of what God is doing among them and among other African churches and other cultures around the world. As I was awestruck by the dynamic power of the Apostles' life in Christ, they were delighted to meet a person from, in John's words, a different language, people, and nation, who could yet speak their language and worship with them around the fiery throne of God's presence. They sensed immediately a mission frontier, a mission opportunity. Encountering the other and being united by Christ with the other is still the dawn we welcome on the horizon of Christian mission, still the pilgrimage we undertake with God within human history and into the consummation of God's work beyond history.

Chapter Three

Mission in History

One of my most vivid experiences of mission history was discovering a historical treasure that had been lost and was on the verge of being destroyed. It was at Bonda, the Anglican mission in the eastern highlands of Zimbabwe where I was an Episcopal missionary with my wife Jane and our four children. As priest among the dozen rural congregations of the Bonda Church District, I was eager to learn about early Christian work in the area. It was amazing to talk with Grandmother Mawadza, who was old enough to remember the founding of St. David's congregation at Bonda by African evangelists in 1908. From catechists Edward Mangwanda and Sylvester Gorogodo I gathered how schools had built up church life and learned how leaders were formed in catechetical training courses. From everyone I heard a great deal about the Liberation War that brought black-majority rule in 1980 and how difficult church life had been during that period. Hearing the history that people had lived helped me understand how they thought about their past, present, and future as Christians in the church. Written records of the history, however, seemed to be in short supply. The church sacristy had service books for the few years just before my time, but nothing from earlier in the century.

Near the church building was an old *imba yakaten-derera*, the round thatched structure so common in southern Africa. No one had been in it for a long time, and the thatch was missing from much of its round peak. One day I opened the rusted door latch and went in. Bits of thatch lay on the floor, along with the debris of years. Above, there was plenty of blue sky visible between the ridge poles. Books piled helter-skelter in two old wooden boxes without lids caught my attention. Sure enough, here were the records—service registers and other books from 1910 on, when St. David's was first assigned a priest by the Anglican Diocese of Southern Rhodesia. Providentially, there was thatch on the roof above where the boxes were sitting, or they would have been destroyed through years of rainy seasons. Why were the books not in a safer place? Maybe during the war, when there was pressure to suspend worship and destroy Christian artifacts, the books had been hurriedly stowed away and then forgotten.

I sat down to read. I read of the travels of Samuel Christelow, an English priest who served Bonda during the 1910s and 20s. There were so few clergy then that the Bonda priest was responsible for scores of far-flung congregations, which he reached by riding on mules for three weeks at a time. Often the register recorded services not in churches but in family home-steads in the bush to which neighbors came to hear the preaching and receive communion. I read of how people from the outlying congregations came in for the great festival of Easter, staying for days at a time, a pattern that continues in the Zimbabwean church today. During the worldwide influenza pandemic of 1918 services were suspended for three months throughout Rhodesia to reduce the chances of infection.

But how had such a vast charge developed in the first place? In the national archives I found a typescript account by George Broderick, Christelow's predecessor, of a mass movement toward Christianity in Manicaland during the early twentieth century. At the time he wrote home to his supporters:

> Here is Church History in the making, being made so rapidly that we hold our breath. It is the work of the people themselves—what will it grow into? Properly guided, efficiently looked after, provided with the means of grace, here is a force being prepared for the evangelisation of the whole country.

Broderick also quotes a missionary colleague:

> Here in Manyikaland it is no longer a question of the conversion of individuals . . . it is the question of the conversion of a district, practically of the people of the Manyika. The movement is obviously of God: we can do, and have done, extraordinarily little. Every tour brings home to me the little we can do. And yet the thing is being done. What we are working for is being accomplished, not by us, but by the Power of God.

Looking back on that period, Broderick wrote:

> Truly the work of the priest was not so much evangelisation, which was being done by the people themselves, but he was continually overwhelmed with shepherding the crowds brought in by those who had glimpsed a little of the Light, and always he was faced with the traveling to be done, mostly on foot, in that roadless and mountainous country.[1]

These observations resonated with my own excitement at witnessing another mass movement into the churches, this one in the new Zimbabwe of the postwar 1980s.

I was struck by how such vital Anglican Christianity had grown from the initial work of a lone bishop, G. W. H. Knight-Bruce, who went into Rhodesia in 1891 with five catechists from Mozambique and South Africa. The bishop's views of Shona culture were scarcely enlightened—he wrote, for instance, "No one who has not had dealings with the really heathen native can credit what a degradation of humanity they are."[2] To the question, "What is the religion of the Mashona?" he replied, "It is very hard to say that they have any.... Their ideas on religion were few and vague."[3] The African catechists had more appreciative attitudes, however, and it was they who carried out the grassroots work of proclaiming the gospel, offering pastoral care and building church communities. The radiant life and sacrificial witness of catechist Bernard Mizeki, the young Mozambican martyred during the 1896 Shona and Ndebele rebellion against the white settlers, was so compelling that today the festival held close to his feast day of June 18 is the largest annual gathering of Anglicans in the world.

This brief glimpse of Anglican Christianity in the last century in one African country highlights several dimensions of the history of Christian mission. First, the history of Christianity is a history of mission. A brochure from the Church Mission Society in Britain asks, "How did the Christian Church become the biggest family on earth?" Our answer should be: Through Christians responding to God's call to mission. Each one of us is the fruit of Christian mission. Some have come to Christ as a new experience through the witness of others in their lives. Those who cannot remember not being Christian were certainly nurtured in faith by parents or other relatives, and somewhere back in the family line some experience of mission prompted in someone a conversion that profoundly affected the descendants. Christian history is the history of a mission movement. Just as there was a mass movement among the Manyika people that echoes today in Zimbabwean church life, there has been a global mass movement that began with Jesus and the apostles and continues in our own day. This is obvious, but it needs emphasis because Christian history is often talked and written about as the history of an institution and its many departments, personalities, and controversies, while the initial gospel proclamation and church-planting are taken for granted. In fact, the nature of the gospel's initial proclamation deeply affects all that follows. If we understand mission as participation in what God is up to in the world, we also realize that the mission story never stops in the later life of a Christian community.

Second, mission history is primarily the story of peoples receiving a mission impulse and making it their own, not primarily the story of outside missionaries and their agencies. George Broderick and his colleague felt like bystanders in a movement of God among the people, a phenomenon quite beyond anything they had asked for or imagined. That is an authentic missionary note throughout Christian history. Individual missionaries have important roles to play, whether in initial proclamation or other service along the way, but as soon as the gospel is embraced the work becomes a collaboration in which the receivers dominate in shaping the movement. It was the African catechist, not the English bishop, who left the deepest mark on Zimbabwean Anglicanism. Christian work at Bonda, now the largest and most multifaceted Anglican mission complex in Zimbabwe, was begun by Shona evangelists. It was ordinary believers who energized the early mass movement, and it was ordinary believers who catalyzed the independence-period revival that I was privileged to witness in Zimbabwe.

Third, mission work has often been distorted by sinful structures of oppression such as imperialism, colonialism, racism, sexism, and sometimes even military coercion. Yet when the gospel is fully received it catalyzes liberation from the very structures in which it was entangled. The Rhodesian colonial regime was racist and also ostensibly Christian. From their own reading of scripture, however, African Christians saw the contradiction, developed a biblical theology of liberation, and began the struggle that eventually brought majority rule. In the life of the church, missionary leaders whose views resembled those of Bishop Knight-Bruce imposed styles and norms of religious life—whether in worship, theology, or ethics—that were ill-suited to the Zimbabwean context. Simultaneously, however, Shona Christians were developing a breathtakingly vital and exuberant church life that is not remotely a carbon copy of what the missionaries brought. This double dynamic of oppression and liberation is crucial to understanding the mission theme in Christian history. We meet arrogant attitudes and oppressive structures in that history, but they are not finally determinative. Missionaries have made mistakes, but they do not have the last word. It is the receivers who hold the real power, and in the cycles of history it is they who shape their Christian life as they make the gospel their own and take control of their churches. Ultimately, the last word lies with the Christ who says, "Behold, I make all things new!" and then proceeds with great regularity to do just that.

With these broad understandings about mission history, we turn to several specific themes. In place of a full-scale chronological review, which the compass of this book does not permit, these themes offer perspective on concerns that people have about mission today and provide an overview of the early, medieval, and pre-modern periods. The themes of this chapter are the gospel's encounter with other religions; the gospel's encounter with human cultures; the role of monasticism among the diverse agencies of Christian mission; and the history of coercion in Christian mission.

∾ Christianity's Encounter with Other Religions

Certainly a major theme at the heart of Christian mission is the encounter with other religions and worldviews. We have seen that any kind of religious mission includes the spiritual vision and practical means through which people project their religious faith and invite the adherence and participation of others. From the first century on, Christian mission has been shaped by the view that what God has done in Christ offers a unique opportunity to all people for reconciliation with God and for fullness of life. The invitation that Christians have extended to others to grow in relationship with Christ has therefore included a premise that the Christian way offers essential possibilities that other religions may not. Today many find this premise problematic. People wonder whether any one religious way can be superior to another, and they see followers of other religions apparently quite fulfilled in their particular paths. This section aims not to resolve this issue but simply to provide a historical perspective on how early Christians approached it in carrying out mission.

Writers in the New Testament both assert that Christ is crucial and recognize points of contact between the gospel and other religious perspectives. "You cannot drink the cup of the Lord and the cup of demons," Paul exclaims to the Corinthians regarding the question of participating in rituals devoted to the Greek gods at Corinth (1 Corinthians 10:21). However, as he ponders the righteousness of Gentiles who never had the law of Moses, Paul suggests to the Romans that apparently righteous Gentiles "show that what the law requires is written on their hearts" (Romans 2:15). Luke's account of Paul's extraordinary appeal on the Areopagus in Athens is based on a perception that even as the Athenians reverenced their pantheon of deities, the Altar to an Unknown God embodied their intuition that there was another way that their own poets and philosophers had anticipated (Acts 17:16-34). Such explorations suggest that other religious approaches offer insights that point toward the gospel even as, in general, the New Testament declares that the pivotal importance of Christ mandates the mission of gospel proclamation and invitation.

Christianity's encounter with other religions close at hand is often discussed today as though it were a new situation for mission. In fact, early Christians affirmed the centrality of Christ in a context of many religious and philosophical options, and their movement grew in that environment. The first century was a cosmopolitan time much like our own, for the ease of travel and communication achieved by the *pax Romana* brought cultural groups into contact with one another and facilitated the spread of religious cults that otherwise would have been confined to local areas. The severe goddess Cybele in Asia Minor (Turkey today) became so popular that the meteor thought to symbolize her was transported to Rome and installed on the Palatine in 204 B.C. The enigmatic cult of Mithras had wide currency among Roman legionnaires. The dramatic liturgies of the Eleusinian mysteries in Greece had drawn a widespread following for fifteen hundred years and continued for several hundred more into the Christian era. The cult of Egypt's Isis as the goddess of all life similarly drew people from throughout the Mediterranean world. Intellectuals discounted these cults as superstition and explored philosophical approaches like Stoicism, which posited a single principle of the universe. On the other hand, astrology was probably the most common practical religion alongside the official cult of the emperor.

In this diverse religious environment, the cult of Jesus of Nazareth was initially just another option jostling in a competitive marketplace, but it grew with astonishing rapidity and power. What was the gospel's appeal in the religiously diverse world of the first century? The monotheistic proclamation of one God was attractive amid the bewildering variety of gods available in Hellenistic culture. Here Christianity borrowed on the already existing attraction of Judaism, which had synagogues in most cities and included seven percent of the empire's population. It is possible that, once it was decided that Gentiles need not first become Jews through circumcision in order to become Christians, Gentiles saw the church as a less burdensome way of participating in the covenant of Abraham. Christians' insistence that Christ was the *only* way of salvation, an exclusivism influenced by the gospel's Jewish roots, contrasted with other cults' easy invitation to mingle devotion to them all, but apparently many found a one-way approach more appealing. People were attracted to Jesus as a real person, rather than as another mythological figure; as the incarnation of God's concern with human beings, different from philosophical speculations; and as a savior whose resurrection conquered sin, death, and oppressive spirits.

Under the scourge of persecution, often inspiring in itself, the new cult celebrated its community life not in public buildings but through small, house-based groups that appealed to many, especially with the Christians' relatively egalitarian attitudes toward women, slaves, and ethnic groups. Commenting on Christians' sacrificial generosity toward one another and toward the poor, the north African theologian Tertullian reported around the year 200 that non-Christians were saying, "See how they love one another and how they are ready to die for each other."[4] The movement spread primarily through the evangelism of its members as they moved about, yet the intentional travel of specially designated missionaries also ensured the movement's wide diffusion. It may have reached India by the year 52 and Britain by 61. It is estimated that by the year 260 forty percent of the empire's population was Christian and that by 300 no part of the empire was entirely unevangelized.[5]

The gospel was offered everywhere as an alternative to other religious ways, and in this period the movement grew rapidly not only without coercion or the promise of material advantage but, indeed, with the major challenge of intermittent and sometimes ferocious persecution. Clearly, a religiously diverse world such as the one we live in today is not a new environment for the gospel, but rather was the home territory in which the gospel first took root and grew. A basic historical fact of Christian mission, then, is that as the gospel has been proclaimed in word and deed people have found it intrinsically compelling enough for them to make the change in life orientation that we call conversion. While conversion in some periods has been influenced by coercion or motives of gain, genuinely religious conversion appears to have been dominant in early Christianity's decisive period of growth.

Adaptation of non-Christian practices and institutions to Christian practice has been common throughout Christian history, and it occupies a mediating position between simple rejection of other religions and a more inquiring and listening stance. Pope Gregory the Great's instructions to Augustine and the other missionaries he sent to evangelize Britain in 596 represent such a mediating position:

> The idol temples of that race should by no means be destroyed, but only the idols in them. Take holy water and sprinkle it in these shrines, build altars and place relics in them. For if the shrines are well built, it is essential that they should be changed from the worship of devils to the service of the true God. When this people see that their shrines are not destroyed they will be able to banish error from their hearts and be more ready to come to the places they are familiar with, but now recognizing and worshiping the true God. And because they are in the habit of slaughtering much cattle as sacrifices to devils, some solemnity ought to be given them in exchange for this.... Thus while some outward rejoicings are preserved, they will be able more easily to share in inward rejoicings.[6]

Gregory believed that such adaptation had ample precedent in ancient Israel, where, he argued, Jewish sacrifices to God were themselves rooted in pagan sacrificial practices.

~ Christianity's Encounter with Diverse Cultures

The gospel's encounter with other religions is related to its encounter with the diversity of human cultures. "In abbreviation," declared Paul Tillich, the twentieth-century theologian, "religion is the substance of culture, culture is the form of religion."[7] Less categorically, we can say that every religious expression is culturally formed, and that culture often expresses religious values, either explicitly or implicitly.

The second-century theologian Justin Martyr is known primarily as an apologist—a polemical defender of the faith—not as a mission figure. However, his zeal for expressing Christian faith through the perspective of classical Greek philosophy established a basis for the now longstanding mission tradition of engaging culture at the level of symbols and meanings. Active in Ephesus and Rome, Justin passed successively through Stoic, Aristotelian, Pythagorean, and Platonist philosophical schools before his conversion. While he then considered other popular religious paths to be sheer superstition, he saw Christianity as "the true philosophy" and connected it with Plato's conceptions of a transcendent God, the soul's relationship with God, human responsibility, and a coming judgment. Justin intended his theology of the incarnation, built on the philosophical concept of the divine *Logos*, or Word, in the prologue to John's gospel, to be intelligible to reason as it was understood in the Hellenistic world. Such rooting of the gospel in the intellectual currents of the time was crucial to the church's mission outreach in the first centuries. Today we realize that the Hellenistic expression of Christian theology, dominant for so long in the West, may not be equally relevant to people in other cultural contexts. Yet as Christians devise new theological formulations that speak to different contexts, we do so on the basis of Justin's principle.

Early Christians were equally aware of discontinuities between the gospel as they understood it and the culture in which they lived. The baptismal instructions recorded in the *Apostolic Tradition* of Hippolytus of Rome, in about the year 215, stipulated not only that prostitutes and their managers must abandon their trade, but also that professions such as teaching children, sculpting stone, acting in dramas, and serving in the military were incompatible with conversion, for these dimensions of culture were steeped in the cults of the Greek and Roman gods. Where popular culture was influenced by a variety of religions, Christians' mission stance was one of critical distance.

How different the situation was two centuries later! Not only was Christianity permitted and popularized through the conversion of the emperor Constantine in 315, but beginning in 391 the emperor Theodosius made Christianity virtually the empire's official religion, with penalties for non-compliance. Pagan sacrifices were outlawed and temples were closed, while the church and its hierarchy were promoted as major institutions of civil society, often with responsibilities for administration. Where polytheism had been linked to patriotism, now Christian profession brought approval, and patronizing the old cults prompted suspicions about one's loyalty to the state. Imperial authorities doubtless saw this as furthering Christ's mission, for vast numbers of people became Christians, at least in name.

This official establishment of Christianity was the foundation of Christendom, which implemented the concept of an earthly kingdom of Christ through the offices of the state and the cultural resources of society. The institution of Christendom in Europe continued without major challenge until the eighteenth-century Enlightenment in the West, and it broke up only in the twentieth century. Vestiges persist today, among them state-established Anglicanism in Britain, the diplomatic status of the Vatican, and a vague but powerful "civil religion" in the United States. Mandatory religious profession was not a Christian innovation, but it attacked directly the principle of voluntary decision implicit in Christ's mission. The New Testament affirms the gospel can positively affect society, but by linking Christianity to state authority Christendom wrenched the church's relationship with culture in ways that have distorted Christian mission down to our own day. As state authority established a Christian dispensation, the spiritual authority of the church, in turn, could be used to stamp particular features of society with divine approval and remove them from scrutiny or challenge. The divine right of monarchs to rule was the most potent instance in medieval Europe, for it invested rulers' political and military decisions with divine authority, along with the economic and social arrangements of the feudal system.

Christendom enmeshed culture, church, and state in a web of mutually reinforcing and imprisoning structures that aggravated the common human tendency to be chauvinistic about one's own culture. The gospel's role of judging all cultures was compromised as one's own culture acquired a bogus aura of divine approval that could be used to condemn whatever was different in other cultures. Cultural imperialism became common in Christian mission, whether in Roman attitudes toward the Germanic tribes, Spanish dealings in Latin America, or modern Euro-American approaches to Africa and Asia.

The attempt to impose one's own cultural norms on others was implemented with the justification of offering "civilization" to those presumed to be "uncivilized." Writing of his mission work in Massachusetts in 1671, Puritan John Eliot declared that the American Indians must be civilized before their conversion could be complete. A century later, William Carey, an English Baptist, launched the modern English-speaking and non-Roman Catholic missionary outreach through his extraordinary venture in Calcutta in 1793. After he began working in India he inquired deeply into Hindu thought and custom, but his famous initial appeal for Protestant mission effort characterized non-western peoples as "poor, barbarous, naked pagans as destitute of civilization as they are of true religion."[8]

In the nineteenth-century heyday of Protestant and Anglican mission, the heads of two major missionary-sending agencies saw danger in identifying Christianity with civilization, but they were confident that civilization would be one fruit of gospel preaching. Rufus Anderson of the American Board of Commissioners for Foreign Mission, which was predominantly Congregational, asked missionaries to concentrate on proclamation, not on education and medicine. Yet he believed that not only western but New England civilization, in particular, was superior to all others. Anglican Henry Venn of the Church of England's Church Missionary Society worked against specific policies of colonial traders and administrators, especially concerning the slave trade, yet he believed that the British Empire's extension was part of a providential ordering of history.

Today we have a greater appreciation for not only the high culture that Justin Martyr was exploring but also the popular culture of ordinary people, and that mission stance does have substantial precedent. In 1622, the pope established the Sacred Congregation for the Propagation of the Faith, often called simply the Propaganda, for "the dissemination of the Christian faith." Its instructions to missionaries in 1649 resonate strongly with views common today:

> Do not regard it as your task, and do not bring any pressure to bear on the peoples, to change their manners, customs, and uses, unless they are evidently contrary to religion and sound morals. What could be more absurd than to transport France, Spain, Italy, or some other European country to China? Do not introduce all that to them, but only the faith, which does not despise or destroy the manners and customs of any people, always supposing that they are not evil, but rather wishes to see them preserved unharmed. . . . Do not draw invidious contrasts between the customs of the people and those of Europe; do your utmost to adapt yourselves to them.[9]

This stance was anticipated and perhaps even informed by the work of the Society of Jesus, or the Jesuits, the missionary order founded by Ignatius of Loyola in 1534, which quickly became a major vehicle of Roman Catholic mission worldwide. In carrying out slow but fruitful evangelism in the Chinese imperial court in the first decade of the 1600s, Mateo Ricci gained acceptance by adopting the vocation and personal style of an aristocratic Chinese scholar. Following Ricci's example in Tamilnadu, South India, Roberto Nobili resolved that to win the Indians he would become an Indian. He made a careful study of Brahman custom and prejudice, and abandoned everything that could offend, such as the eating of meat and the wearing of leather shoes. He adopted the ochre *(kavi)* robe of the holy man, and as far as could be converted himself in a *sannyasi guru*, a teacher who has renounced every form of attachment to the world. He mastered classical Tamil. To this he was later able to add Telugu and Sanscrit.[10]

During the twentieth century, the erosion of the intellectual basis and practical arrangements of Christendom enabled the mission movement—Anglican, Roman Catholic, and Protestant—to recover the spirit of these early Jesuits. The movement began to appreciate and explore the new gospel expressions emerging from the cultural diversity of Christian faith and community worldwide.

∼ The Monastic Contribution to Mission

Christian mission has from its beginning been carried out through a wide variety of agencies or means, and the early modes have served as exemplars ever since. Jesus modeled the visionary individual, but simultaneously he gathered and trained a company of fellow missioners, and the women who supported them can be seen as the first missionary support society. In commissioning Paul and Barnabas for their mission to the nations, the community in Antioch became the first church explicitly to send out missionaries. During his travels Paul sought to establish the principle that the itinerant missionary could expect financial support from congregations committed to the work. Important as such missioners were in setting the vision and venturing into new territories, the bulk of Christian mission was carried out by ordinary believers in the course of daily life in their migrations around the Mediterranean world.

Monastic communities have played a major role in Christian mission since the blossoming of monasticism in the fifth and sixth centuries. In seeking to create a Christian society, Christendom had collapsed the tension between gospel and culture and compromised the gospel's ability to critique popular norms. After the conversion of Constantine in the fourth century, Christians who had lived their faith as a costly way of discipleship over against the culture and the state began to see thousands around them adopting Christian identity as a convenient label with no genuine conversion, sacrifice, or faithfulness. Disillusionment with such nominal Christianity stimulated the monastic movement, through which people sought to be Christian with single-minded and counter-cultural devotion. By their very nature, monasteries separated themselves from "the world," but the attention monks and nuns paid to the counsels of scripture prompted them to offer proclamation and compassion to those in their immediate neighborhoods and to propagate the gospel to peoples in other lands.

Through incessant evangelistic and pastoral work as a bishop, Patrick moved the people of Ireland from being essentially non-Christian in 430 to being largely Christian by 460. He also laid the foundations of the Celtic monasticism that nurtured, among many other initiatives, Columba's mission work in Scotland from the island of Iona. Pope Gregory the Great sent Benedictine monks to Britain as missionaries in 596, for he felt that the contemplative life must bear fruit in action. The conversion of Germany in the eighth century was advanced largely by Boniface, consecrated bishop in 722 not to a particular see, but with a mandate to preach to non-Christian Germans; his most celebrated act was felling the sacred oak of Thor at Geismar in Hesse in 724. An English monk, Boniface was influenced by Gregory's activist interpretation of the monastic vocation, and his strategy of establishing monasteries to support mission bore the marks of Irish influence in England.

Much of the burden of later Roman Catholic mission was carried by the two orders of friars, the Franciscans and the Dominicans. Perhaps the most admired of all saints, Francis of Assisi (1181-1226) was concerned that Christ's love reach the poor through a witness of simplicity and joy, and before the end of the thirteenth century Franciscans were found throughout the world as then known by Europeans. The concern of Francis's contemporary Peter Dominic was preaching for the conversion of heretics. His Order of Preachers, as the Dominicans were known, was soon similarly dispersed, making strong contributions in education, although they also assisted in notorious inquisitions against heretics during the following two centuries. Orthodox mission was advanced by monks in the medieval and modern periods through the work of missionaries such as Stephen of Perm, a Russian Orthodox monk who worked among the Zyrians of the north European forests in the fourteenth century. Although not a monastic order, the Jesuits, as already noted, were a major factor in Roman Catholic mission from the time of the Counter-Reformation of the sixteenth century, and they have been followed by numerous other missionary orders in the modern period, such as the Missionaries of Africa and the Maryknolls.

The Anglo-Catholic revival of the mid-nineteenth century brought monasticism back into Anglicanism, and Anglican orders soon felt called to mission out-reach. Bernard Mizeki was baptized in 1886 through the ministry of the Society of St. John the Evangelist (SSJE), the first modern Anglican order, at St. Philip's Church in Capetown, South Africa, and the American house of SSJE later had a community in Japan. The Community of the Resurrection, based in Mirfield, England, has long been active in southern Africa, where Trevor Huddleston became well known for his witness against apartheid. The Boston-based American convent of the Society of St. Margaret initiated a variety of ministries in Haiti that have become major institutions of the Episcopal diocese in that country. The Order of the Holy Cross, founded in the United States, now has a monastery in South Africa. Cross-cultural witness has thus been a natural fruit of monastic communities' commitment to be faithful to the whole of Christ's mission.

～ Coercion in the Name of Mission

The dark side of Christian mission is the history of force exerted to coerce peoples to adopt Christianity as their creed and religion. The history offers such blatant examples that the very notion of Christian mission is linked inextricably in the minds of many people today with the notion of forcing people to become Christian and a general impression of "pushiness."

Christendom, again, provided the intellectual framework and the practical arrangements for coercive mission. Christendom conceived Christian profession as not only a personal decision but a national commitment, and it lodged in the state a responsibility for ensuring religious conformity among both its own citizens and newly subject peoples. This view of the state's relation to religion was not a Christian invention but was simply taken over from longstanding assumptions of the Greco-Roman order. Citizens of Athens, for instance, were obliged to honor Athena, and the cult of the Roman emperor was obligatory throughout the empire, alongside whatever other religious interests and loyalties a person might have. Christians were victims of this rule as they experienced persecution under the Romans, but when the emperor adopted Christianity it was a natural cultural reflex to assume that the new religion should be promulgated as an obligation. The exclusivist heritage of Judaism, the Old Testament's strictures against paganism, and the New Testament's apparently exclusivist view of Jesus led to this promulgation being implemented in ways that were stricter than those of, say, the old imperial cult. It was a natural enculturation of the gospel in a period when monarchs assumed the right to exercise absolute power in all areas of life.

It was all quite natural—and tragic in its distortion of the gospel. By 450 the chief mode of conversion was of entire peoples led by their monarchs. The baptism of Clovis, king of the Franks, in 496 brought that major Germanic group into the Christian fold. Under Charlemagne, king of the Franks from 771 to 814, the Christian realm was often extended through conquering German tribes, whose conversion was included in the terms of peace. Draconian laws sought to enforce Christian profession and practice, as in these rules for the Saxons:

> Any unbaptized Saxon who attempts to hide himself among his own people and refuses to accept baptism shall be put to death. . . . Anyone who burns the body of a dead person, as is the pagan fashion, shall be put to death.[11]

The "Christianization" of peoples often served primarily political and economic interests, but it is important to note that genuinely religious mission was occurring simultaneously, as we saw with Boniface. In the case of Charlemagne, his adviser Alcuin of York criticized the entire policy toward the Saxons, arguing that mission should proceed by preaching and systematic teaching, not by simply baptizing people who had no knowledge of the faith.

The principal external challenge to Christendom was the rise of Islam, beginning with Muhammad's pilgrimage from Mecca to Medina in 622. "There is no God but God, and Muhammad is the prophet of God" became the proclamation of a vigorously missionary religion that carried out its own military campaigns uniting Arabia, then conquering Palestine and Syria by 640, Persia by 650, and north Africa by 700. The eastern churches survived under Muslim rule, but with progressively reduced influence down to the fall of Constantinople in 1453. Recovering the Christian holy sites from the hands of the Muslims in Palestine was the rationale for the Crusades, the succession of military campaigns launched over two centuries by popes and western European rulers. The infamous savageries perpetrated on the assumption that members of another religious group had no right to live are probably the events cited most frequently in critique of Christian mission. Writes mission historian Stephen Neill:

> And so, for the two centuries that elapsed between the first conquest of Jerusalem in 1099, and the loss of the last Crusader stronghold at Acre in 1291, the Mediterranean world was darkened by an ever more sombre cloud of hatred, all the more disastrous because this hate

was conjured up in the name of Christ. In three ways the Crusades have left an almost indelible stain on Christian history. They permanently injured the relations between the Western and the Eastern branches of Christendom.... The Crusades left a trail of bitterness across the relations between Christians and Muslims that remains as a living factor in the world situation to the present day.... Thirdly, the Crusades involved a lowering of the whole moral temperature of Christendom.[12]

The Crusades illustrate the malignant power of Christendom's alliance of church and state to promote a profoundly mistaken religious enthusiasm that, in return, authorized deadly military force in the interests of ethnocentric prejudice.

The military campaigns of the *conquistadors* in Central and South America demonstrated that the failure of the Crusades was followed by a failure to learn from them. When, as a result of Columbus's voyage in 1492, Pope Alexander VI presumed to divide between Portugal and Spain the lands of which Europe was newly aware, he charged their monarchs

to bring to Christian faith the peoples who inhabit these islands and the mainland . . . and to send to the said islands and to the mainland wise, upright, God-fearing, and virtuous men who will be capable of instructing the indigenous peoples in good morals and in the Catholic faith.[13]

In 1503 Queen Isabella of Spain directed that the Indians on the island of Hispaniola—today divided between Haiti and the Dominican Republic—be both evangelized and enlisted to work in the mines, but without slavery. The Dominican priest Bartolomé de Las Casas reported in 1640 that, instead, the forced labor conditions imposed by the Spanish were so brutal that

> the multitude of people who originally lived on this island, which according to the admiral, was infinite . . . was consumed at such a rate that in those eight years [following 1503] ninety percent had perished. From here this sweeping plague went to San Juan, Jamaica, Cuba and the continent, spreading destruction over the whole hemisphere.[14]

De Las Casas himself had undergone a change of heart before he became a prophetic voice against the catastrophe, but by then the damage had been done. It is with sober repentance that we must acknowledge the same of many incidents in mission history: the damage has been done.

Learning from this history and seeking to reconcile the relationships still wounded by such legacies must be high on the mission agenda. It is humbling to witness sometimes how the sins of the past need not imprison those whose forebears were the victims. While teaching a seminary class in 1992 on contemporary issues in world Christianity, I devoted one session to the implications of that year's five hundredth anniversary of Columbus's arrival in the Americas. A majority of the class, who were white and privileged, believed the occasion should be one of mourning and repentance. One member of the class was from the American southwest and embodied in his person black, Native American, and Hispanic ancestry. "I think the Quincentennial is something to celebrate," he said, "and I intend to celebrate it as the five hundredth anniversary of the arrival of the Christian gospel in the Americas." Although he was aware of the difficult history and its effects on his own ancestors, he nevertheless was resolved not to be bound by the tragedies of the past. It was a decision that was peculiarly his to make, and I respected him for it. At the same time, we must ensure that the future of Christian mission is informed by the record of its past.

It is well to end this reflection with the encouragement that, in the midst of developments that grieve us still, mission history is replete with bright lights who feared not to stand against powers and principalities for an authentic and empowering vision of liberation and fulfillment in Christian mission. One such light was Arthur Shearly Cripps, a British priest in Rhodesia from 1901 to 1953. Initially he was sent through the Society for the Propagation of the Gospel, but he later renounced connection with any missionary society. Committed to the example of Francis of Assisi, Cripps identified deeply with the poor of the land to which he had gone. He insisted on living in a round thatched home, and he traveled everywhere on foot rather than by automobile. Incensed by Rhodesian oppression of African peasants, Cripps campaigned constantly on their behalf in diocesan synods, in the legislature, and in the popular press in matters such as taxation, residential regulations, and, most important, the allocation of land. With his own resources he bought farms for people to settle on, and the church he built he called *Maronda Mashanu*, the Five Wounds. Of his own bishop, he wrote on one occasion:

> The Bishop emphatically denies that there was oppression of the native races, who, he declared, "were dealt with in that spirit of even-handed justice for which the flag of Britain stands." God

forgive him if he really said that. Would it possibly help the Native Cause if I challenged him to disown or withdraw this statement, or if he would do neither, to take three months notice from me?

Alongside the struggle for justice, it was Cripps's personal compassion that endeared him to the Zimbabwean people:

There is a story, vouched for by Canon Christelow, of Cripps conducting a funeral service for a poor African and as he came to that point in the service where the body of the deceased is tenderly laid in the open grave, he reached around to the family for the folded blanket that it was customary to place in the grave as a pillow for the head of the departed one. The family was so poor that they had no blanket to give, so Cripps quietly took off his cassock, folded it up, gave it to be used as a pillow in the grave, and went on to take the service in his shirt sleeves.[15]

It is such witness that made Cripps so widely known, along with Bernard Mizeki, in Zimbabwean Anglican history. Alongside the dark side of mission, such witness is also part and parcel of the story.

Chapter Four

The Anglican and Episcopal Mission Story

Profound insights about Christian faith and mission are embodied in the statues above the main entrance on the west front of London's Westminster Abbey, probably the best known Anglican monument in the world. Ten niches were included in the entrance when it was built in the fifteenth century, but, strangely, they were never filled with statues as were the many niches elsewhere in the edifice. When, in 1973, a major restoration of the abbey was launched, filling the empty niches was included in the project.

Whom should the statues commemorate? The abbey was already well known for hundreds of statues representing biblical figures, saints, bishops, poets, and other luminaries such as David Livingstone, the nineteenth-century English missionary-explorer. It was decided that the new sculptures should highlight the fact that the twentieth century saw not only more innocent suffering but also more Christian martyrdoms than any other century, including the church's early periods of persecution. Accordingly, ten twentieth-century martyrs are depicted in the statuary.

Representing various parts of the world, they are persons whose witness is affirmed by Christians in their regions and who can inspire all in the global Christian community.

Four of the ten statues represent martyrs in the traditionally Christian areas of the Global North. The Grand Duchess Elizabeth, who had Lutheran and Anglican backgrounds alongside her Orthodox faith, was killed in 1918 with other members of Russia's royal family. In 1941, Maximilian Kolbe, a Roman Catholic priest, stepped forward in the Auschwitz concentration camp to take the place of another prisoner, who was married with children and who was one of ten arbitrarily picked for execution after a prisoner escaped. Dietrich Bonhoeffer, the Lutheran theologian, was hanged in Flossenburg concentration camp by the Nazis in 1945 for his part in resisting Hitler's regime. Martin Luther King, Jr., an American and a Baptist, was assassinated in 1968 during the civil rights struggle in the American south.

The other six statues represent martyrs from Africa, Asia, Latin America, and Oceania, parts of the world that earlier were mission frontiers for churches of the Global North. These six witness to the fresh vitality of the Christianity that has grown up in those areas. Three of this group were not Anglicans. In 1960, Qamar Zia, a young Pakistani woman who took the name of Esther John, was bludgeoned in her sleep by assailants presumed to be family members objecting to her Christian conversion and her refusal to marry a Muslim. Oscar Romero, the Roman Catholic archbishop of El Salvador, spoke out against government-sponsored human rights abuses and was shot in 1980 as he celebrated mass. In 1973, during China's Cultural Revolution, pastor Wang Zhiming of the Christian Three-Self Patriotic Movement was executed before a crowd of ten thousand, most of them Christians forced to attend to frighten them into renouncing their faith.

The statues of three Anglican martyrs from the Two-Thirds World highlight the complex results of Anglican mission. Manche Masemola, a fifteen-year-old girl of the Pedi people of Sekhukhuneland in South Africa, was beaten to death in 1928—by her parents, according to an eyewitness—when she refused to renounce her Christian faith and practice. Whereas in China Christianity was experienced by Wang Zhiming's minority Miao people as affirming their local culture over against the Communist regime, the Pedi in South Africa connected Christianity with the colonialism that was undermining their political and cultural autonomy. Anglican mission work among the Pedi continued to grow only slowly after the martyrdom, and in 1969 Manche Masemola's mother was baptized after almost forty years of opposing Christians and denying responsibility for her daughter's death. Today hundreds gather at Manche Masemola's grave for the annual celebration of her martyrdom.

Lucian Tapiedi is regarded by Anglicans in Papua New Guinea virtually as their patron saint. A teacher and evangelist from among the Massim people, he was hacked to death in 1942 by other Papuans who feared reprisals by the Japanese invaders if they harbored missionaries or their associates. Tapiedi's father had been a sorcerer, but his mother converted to Christianity and dedicated her two sons to the church. In the midst of intensive effort by so many mission groups that Papua New Guinea has the highest missionaries-to-population ratio in the world (1:1430), Anglican and Roman Catholic missioners have generally affirmed indigenous culture and religion more than have their evangelical counterparts. It is striking that Tapiedi's murderer, having escaped retribution, later converted to Christianity, took the name Lucian at his baptism, and built a church dedicated to "St. Lucian Tapiedi."

Janani Luwum, Anglican archbishop of Uganda, Rwanda, Burundi, and Boga-Zaire, was executed in 1976 in retaliation for his criticism of Idi Amin, the brutal dictator of Uganda from 1971 to 1979. Converted through the witnessing and confessing Christianity known as the East African Revival, or the *abalokol*, Luwum was a visionary dedicated to nurturing the "spiritual selfhood" of African Christianity. "In short," he said,

> this means that our talented Ugandan men and women who have been imbued with the Spirit of the Living God should begin to express themselves in Music, Art, Drama, Literature and other creative forms in order to revive our valuable cultural and traditional heritage so that the Christian Gospel can be communicated at a level our people can easily grasp.[1]

Today Uganda alone, with its 7.4 million Anglicans, constitutes the third largest province in the Anglican Communion, after England and Nigeria.

The abbey statues say a good deal about the global Christianity that mission work has built over the past centuries. Just four out of the ten statues represent the traditionally Christian Global North, with the Orthodox and Roman Catholic communions represented alongside the Lutheran and Baptist churches. The six from the Global South testify to the shift in Christianity's center of gravity to Africa, Asia, and Latin America. Here Roman Catholicism, the world's largest church with more than one billion members, is

represented once more in Oscar Romero. Non-denom-
inational Protestantism is represented by Esther John,
who was hosted by Anglicans and Presbyterians at
various times but seems not to have had a denominational affiliation. Wang Zhiming represents "post-
denominational" Christianity in China during the
Communist period, when many traditional churches
merged in the China Christian Council. These seven
statues express Anglicanism's ecumenical spirit of
affirming other churches and emerging forms that
transcend denominational distinctions. The fact that
the three Anglicans are from Asia, Africa, and Oceania
highlights Anglicanism's decisive shift toward the
Global South.

Equally important, the complexity of Christian
martyrdom in the ten stories illuminates the complexity of incarnational Christian faith in the world and
the complexity of mission. The political dimensions of
most of these martyrs enabled their persecutors to
claim that they died not for religious conviction but
for political activity. Similar ambiguity has attended
the deaths of most martyrs in Christian history. The
church, by contrast, knows that political engagement
is among the fruits of genuine faith, and it declares
that these persons were killed on account of their
Christian conviction as understood in a holistic framework.

This ambiguity of martyrdom has an analogy in
the ambiguity of Christian mission. We have seen that
mission in ancient and medieval times was a complex
enterprise, mixing unworthy motives and holy vision,
mutual relationships and racist condescension, military violence and sacrificial service. Ambiguity characterized mission in the modern period, as well. For
instance, the imperial basis of Roman Catholic mission
in the Latin America that later produced Oscar

Romero was echoed in the nineteenth-century imperial entanglement of Europe and North America in mission to the China that later produced Wang Zhiming. Ambiguity is inevitable in living incarnationally in the real world. Discounting the martyrs on account of the complexity of their lives and contexts would be a failure of discernment. Discounting Christians and churches around the world because they are the fruits of flawed Christian mission, Anglican or otherwise, would be a similar failure of discernment. Just as the ten individuals stand out clearly as martyrs for the sake of Christ, so also the Christian communities that grew from the mixed wheat and weeds of Christian mission stand on their own as churches that offer unique gifts to global Christianity and the world's religious life. It is with this affirmation that we turn specifically to the history of Anglican and Episcopal mission.

∿ The Voluntary Principle in Anglican Mission

After the Reformation of the 1500s, two centuries passed before Protestant and Anglican churches expressed substantial interest in mission beyond their own nations in Europe and Britain. The initial preoccupations of the reformed churches crowded out concern for cross-cultural mission. Military conflicts between Protestant and Catholic powers in Europe threatened Protestant survival until the Peace of Westphalia in 1648. Conflicts among varieties of Protestants also consumed energy, as we know from religious refugees such as Puritans and Quakers who fled England to settle in North America. The continuing pattern of state churches limited mission vision as Anglican and Lutheran rulers focused on securing their borders and ensuring religious consensus within those borders, not on reaching the non-Christians beyond. The high seas were controlled by Spain and Portugal, with the result that Roman Catholic mission accompanied the imperial projects of those powers in Latin America, the Far East, and parts of Africa.

Protestants initially espoused a theology that actually made global mission superfluous. When Baron Justinian von Welz, an Austrian Lutheran, published in 1644 the first significant Protestant argument *for* world mission, he questioned several prevailing Protestant views: that the mission mandate was intended only for the apostles of Jesus; that the gospel may not be preached again where its light has once been extinguished; that ordained ministers are called to serve their congregations, not proclaim the gospel to non-Christians; and, in an argument still common today, that preaching abroad should not happen until Christianity is strengthened at home. He wrote passionately:

> I ask, who gave you authority to misinterpret the commandment of Christ in Matthew 28? . . . I ask you, from 1 Thessalonians 1.8, if ye have brought it about that the Word of God has sounded farther than in Germany and Sweden and Denmark, as Paul so highly commends his Thessalonians that their faith toward God is gone forth from them into all places?[2]

The first major Protestant initiative stemmed from the Pietist movement centered at Halle in Germany, from where, in 1706, Bartholomew Ziegenbalg and Henry Plutschau went to the Danish settlement of Tranquebar on the southeast coast of India. There they developed important mission patterns such as educating new converts in schools, translating scripture into vernacular languages, studying indigenous religion, nurturing personal conversion, and training indigenous pastors. The Moravians, a Pietist group guided by Count Nicolaus von Zinzendorf, began their global work in the 1730s, when they sent missionaries to Greenland and the West Indies. Protestant efforts gathered momentum as England and Holland became maritime powers interested in colonizing the world, but it took time for a mission theology to develop.

The state-established Church of England long displayed little concern for evangelizing non-Christians. Founded in 1607, the Virginia Colony consisted largely of Anglican church members, but it suffered from a clergy shortage, and the Archbishop of Canterbury never provided a bishop for the American colonies. Meanwhile the British East India Company, established in 1600, provided chaplaincy to its own officials but discouraged missionary work with Indians for fear (well founded, as it turned out!) that Christian teaching would prompt unrest among subject peoples and subvert colonial control.

With such lack of official interest in church life and work beyond Britain, it was the initiative of concerned individuals that prompted Anglican mission outreach. In the 1690s, English rector Thomas Bray was asked to help organize Anglican work in Maryland. Anticipating the needs of colonial clergy, in 1698 he and four laymen established the Society for Promoting Christian Knowledge (SPCK), which grew rapidly to become a major book distributor and publisher. With branches today in Australia, India, Ireland, New Zealand, and the United States, it has participated in publishing over two hundred translations of *The Book of Common Prayer* into other languages.

Bray founded yet another group in 1701, the Society for the Propagation of the Gospel in Foreign

Parts (SPG), which was intended both to minister to Britons overseas and to evangelize non-Christians living under the British crown. Formed as a Society by Royal Charter, the SPG had state recognition and official position in the church, but it needed to raise its own funds. It became a major missionary-sending agency with an initial focus on the American colonies, where it worked with American Indians and African Americans and founded some of the oldest parishes of what is now the Episcopal Church. Gradually its work spread: to the West Indies in 1712, Ghana in 1751, Canada in 1759, Australia in 1793, India and South Africa in 1821, and so throughout much of the world. In 1965, it merged with the Universities Mission to Central Africa, the society founded in 1857 through the initiative of David Livingstone, to become the United Society for the Propagation of the Gospel (USPG). Since the Anglo-Catholic revival of the nineteenth century, the society has promoted a high church style of Anglicanism. As a result, Anglicans in areas of SPG work—southern Africa, for instance— tend to enjoy incense and bells in their worship and exercise caution about ecumenical cooperation; they have also been slower in affirming the ordination of women to the priesthood.

The nineteenth-century blossoming of Anglican and Protestant mission work was energized by the founding of more "voluntary societies"—the fruit of a general evangelical awakening in the eighteenth century. They are termed "voluntary" because they were founded, organized, and funded by interested individuals, not by the governing central structures of churches. Concerned that the Church of England continued to be relatively inactive in world mission, a group of Anglican evangelicals known as the Clapham Sect founded the Church Missionary Society (CMS) in

1799. Best known among them was William Wilberforce, who as a member of Parliament was active in the abolition of the slave trade and slavery itself in the British Empire. The CMS both addressed these injustices in the international system and pursued world evangelization with a vision that such work was a prelude to the inauguration of God's kingdom in a coming millennial age.

Whereas the SPG was chartered to operate within areas of British rule, the CMS sought to initiate work outside the British colonial structure and so express the universality of mission. It worked extensively in China, Japan, Persia, the Middle East, India, and west and east Africa. While initially distrusted as an autonomous society, by the mid-1800s the CMS had the support of numerous bishops and was infusing world mission into the ethos of the Church of England. Consistent with its evangelical roots and in contrast with the SPG, the CMS promoted a low church style of Anglicanism. As a result, Anglicans in areas of CMS work—east Africa, for instance—tend to be more revivalist, less centered on the eucharist, and more affirming of the ordination of women.

What perspectives guided the missionary work of such societies? The major policy-maker in nineteenth-century English mission was Henry Venn, secretary of the CMS from 1841 to 1872. His working principles for missionaries included preaching the cross of Christ, learning local languages, translating scripture into the vernacular, providing schools, and cooperating with Protestant denominations. Keenly aware of the twin perils of missionary paternalism and indigenous dependency, Venn counseled missionaries to develop local leadership that would enable new churches to stand on their own as soon as possible. He is best known for setting forth as a chief goal "establishing a Native Church upon the principles of self-support, self-government, and self-extension." These "Three-Self Principles" anticipated by more than a century a current view that missionaries should work themselves out of a job. Strikingly, Venn recommended for each local effort what he called the "euthanasia of a mission":

> It is important ever to keep in view what has been happily termed "the Euthanasia of a Mission" where the Missionary is surrounded by well-trained Native congregations under Native Pastors, when he gradually and wisely abridges his own labours, and relaxes his super-intendence over the Pastors till they are able to sustain their own Christian ordinances, and the District ceases to be a Missionary field, and passes into Christian parishes under the consti-tuted ecclesiastical authorities.[3]

Equally important, Venn expressed a broad consensus of mission leaders at the time that authentic church life among newly evangelized peoples would express their cultural particularities and should not be expect-ed to reproduce the church life of the missionaries, whether Anglican or otherwise.

It was such principles that prompted the CMS to initiate the first mission venture to be directed by an African bishop. Consecrated in 1864 as the first non-European bishop of the Anglican Communion, Samuel Adjai Crowther, a former slave, developed church work in the Niger River delta in eastern Nigeria. In the imperial heyday of the "Scramble for Africa" that commenced in 1885, however, Henry Venn's succes-sors were not nearly so open to indigenous leadership, and the three bishops who followed Bishop Crowther in the Niger region after his death in 1891 were all

Europeans. In the chapel at Partnership House in London, Crowther is depicted in stained glass, alongside three other pioneering indigenous bishops of Anglican churches with which both the CMS and the SPG were involved: Vedanayakam Samuel Azariah of South India, Tsae Seng Sing of China, and Joseph Sakunoshin Motoda of Japan. A number of other mission groups also initiated vigorous work, most notably the South American Missionary Society, founded in 1844.

While today the British societies are smaller than they once were, the spread of Anglicanism around the world was due chiefly to their work. This says several important things about Anglican mission history. First, Anglicanism was spread not by top-down policies of the Church of England hierarchy but by the initiative of grassroots groups that were passionate about mission and that developed networks of support at the parish level. Genuine mission vision, not sheer ecclesiastical ambition, is responsible for the existence of the Anglican Communion. Second, because these groups were voluntary rather than official, they were able to preserve their activism and their particular theological, geographic, and strategic emphases from being blunted by competing priorities in central church structures. This accounts for the staying power of Anglican mission over the last three centuries. Third, in the context of the Church of England's state-established link with a major colonial power, the fact that mission was carried out by the societies rather than by official church structures preserved a critical distance between mission work and colonial policy. Anglican mission was not simply the religious instrument of British imperialism.

∿ The Episcopal Missionary Church Model

Up the street where I minister in Cambridge, Massachusetts, is a vivid reminder of the challenges the Episcopal Church faced in forging an Anglican identity in the new United States. Christ Church, the first Anglican parish in our fair city, was built in 1761 across from Cambridge Common and Harvard College. The state-established character of the Church of England meant that most Anglicans were loyal to the British crown, praying weekly for the king and royal family. Thus the anti-British fervor that soon engulfed the colonies had religious as well as political repercussions for Anglicans. "At the time of the Revolution," notes a historical plaque on the church, "most of the congregation followed the British army to Nova Scotia, and the building was used by General Washington to shelter troops. George and Martha Washington worshipped here on December 31, 1775." That occasion was one of just a handful of services held between 1774 and 1790. When a British soldier was buried in the parish crypt in 1777, outraged townspeople vandalized the church, and it was left open to the elements until repairs were made in 1790. Even then, worship was sustained only by student lay readers and supply clergy, and a rector was not in place until 1839.

For Anglicans living in such widespread disfavor, establishing the Episcopal Church as an autonomous body, not governed from England and yet in full communion with the Archbishop of Canterbury, was a survival strategy motivated by their desire both to maintain Anglican worship and to be accepted as loyal citizens of the new United States. This American innovation formed the first non-British province of what came to be known as the Anglican Communion and established what has become the communion's distinctive pattern of relationships: full local autonomy in legislative decision-making; full inter-provincial communion, united through the Archbishop of Canterbury; and committed consultation, carried out since 1867 chiefly through the Lambeth Conference of bishops. Beyond survival, the American experience was a breakthrough for Anglican mission, for it created the concept of indigenous Anglican Christianity outside Britain. The consecration of Samuel Seabury as the first American bishop in 1784 was followed by an act of Parliament in 1786 that authorized the consecration in England of bishops for dioceses abroad.

However innovative, the new American church was so small and weak that one historian dubbed the period 1789-1835 as "The Church Convalescent"![4] Numbering in 1800 just twelve thousand out of a national population of four million, Episcopalians in the early years focused first on stabilizing their existence as a church, not on mission. They adapted *The Book of Common Prayer* to the American situation, obtained their first bishops, organized dioceses, and established a form of government that was new to Anglicanism. With General Convention modeled on the United States Congress, Episcopal polity from the beginning was more clearly and more centrally organized than in the Church of England. Included with clergy in the House of Deputies, laypeople exercised a church-wide role that their counterparts in Britain did not begin to have until 1885, so that all orders of ministry were formally included in Episcopal decision-making. This centralized, inclusive, and democratic polity was a fundamental condition for the two new modes of mission that developed in the American church: the church-wide missionary society and the appointment of missionary bishops.

The western frontier of the growing nation was the initial mission horizon for Episcopalians, and it widened slowly to include the world. The 1792 General Convention adopted a short-lived plan to raise funds "for supporting missionaries to preach the Gospel on the frontiers," but most of the early work was carried out by diocesan committees. The global horizon was highlighted by Protestant developments and by encouragement from England. Influenced by the first and second Great Awakenings of the 1740s and early 1800s, fledgling Protestant interest in world mission issued in the founding of the American Board of Commissioners for Foreign Missions in 1810 and the Baptist Board of Foreign Missions in 1814. From 1815 on, the Church Missionary Society urged the Episcopal Church to promote world mission, termed "the advancement of the Kingdom of Christ among the heathen." Africa became one focus of interest through the Liberia project of the American Colonization Society, founded in 1816 to help freed slaves return to that continent.

The Domestic and Foreign Missionary Society (DFMS) as established by the 1821 General Convention initially combined the voluntary and centralized modes of missionary support, for it was an official organ of the church, but members paid voluntary dues. After this version of the DFMS proved to have little appeal, the 1835 General Convention took the major step of amending the DFMS constitution to read, "The Society shall be considered as comprehending all persons who are members of this Church."[5] Although certainly solving the membership problem, this change had a strong theological motivation, as expressed at the time by George Washington Doane, bishop of New Jersey, to the DFMS directors:

In an address of great power, he argued "that by the original constitution of Christ, the Church as the Church, was the one great Missionary Society; and the Apostles, and the Bishops, their successors, his perpetual trustees; and this great trust could not, and should never be divided or deputed." The duty, he maintained, to support the Church in preaching the Gospel to every creature, was one which passed on *every Christian by terms of his baptismal vow,* and from which he could never be absolved.[6]

Legislating that every Episcopalian was—and still is today!—a member of the Domestic and Foreign Missionary Society emphasized that the church as a whole is called to mission, which defines the church's nature. Thus mission cannot be delegated to one part of the church, still less to the purely voluntary inclinations of some of its members. Instead it must be embraced by the whole church and expressed through the missionary activity of each of its baptized members. Here we see strong precedent for today's emphasis on baptismal mission and on the missional nature of the church.

Reinforcing also today's recognition that local and global concerns are interrelated and equally important, the 1835 DFMS constitution declared the unity of the mission field:

For the guidance of the Committees [for Domestic Missions and for Foreign Missions] it is declared that the missionary field is always to be regarded as one, THE WORLD—the terms domestic and foreign being understood as terms of locality adopted for convenience. *Domestic* missions are those which are established *within,* and *foreign* missions are those that are established *without*, the territory of the United States.[7]

This insistence on the unity of mission contrasted with the exclusive emphases of British societies, with some devoted to domestic concerns and others to foreign.

Creating the office of missionary bishop—a bishop sent to establish the church in a particular area—was the third major contribution of the 1835 General Convention. Laying the theological foundation of this innovation, Doane declared that a missionary bishop

> is a bishop *sent forth* by the Church, *not sought for* of the Church; going before to organize the Church, not waiting till the Church has partially been organized; a leader not a follower, in the march of the Redeemer's conquering and triumphant Gospel . . . sent by the Church, even as the Church is sent by Christ.[8]

In addition to stressing the apostolic role of a bishop as one sent to preach the gospel, this innovation was premised on the view that the presence of a bishop means that the church itself is present and that a bishop in such circumstances has authority to "grow the church" from that simple fact of presence. As a voluntary society, the CMS, by contrast, believed that the episcopate should be the culmination, not the foundation, of church growth and that, in any case, the first bishop should be an indigenous Christian, not a missionary.

The 1835 convention employed the new office first to build the church's work on the western frontier and elected missionary bishops for the northwest and southwest. Jackson Kemper (now commemorated in the Episcopal calendar on 24 May) was consecrated at the convention as the first missionary bishop, and through his constant travels he laid the foundations of the Episcopal Church in Missouri, Indiana, Iowa, Wisconsin, Minnesota, Nebraska, and Kansas. The first missionary bishop with a non-American jurisdiction was William Boone, elected in 1844 to be bishop of "Amoy and Other Parts of China," where Episcopal missionaries had first arrived in 1835. Liberia, where the DFMS sent missionaries in 1835 and 1836, received a missionary bishop in 1851 and its first African American missionary bishop, Samuel Ferguson, in 1884. In Japan, the third major area of nineteenth-century Episcopal mission, the three Episcopal missionaries who arrived in 1859 were the first non-Roman Catholic Christian missionaries in that country's history, and Channing Moore Williams (commemorated on 2 December) became missionary bishop in 1866.

An extraordinary missionary bishop was Samuel Isaac Joseph Shereschewsky (commemorated on 14 October), whose story illustrates both remarkable mission achievement and the appeal of Anglicanism to pilgrims whose journey is cosmopolitan and interreligious. Born a Lithuanian Jew, Shereschewsky studied to become a rabbi. While pursuing graduate work in Germany, however, he became interested in Christianity through missionaries of the London Society for Promoting Christianity Amongst the Jews, a voluntary ecumenical group. In 1854 he emigrated to the United States, where he studied for the Presbyterian ministry before becoming an Episcopalian and graduating from The General Theological Seminary in New York in 1859. Responding to Boone's call for helpers in China, he learned to write Chinese onboard ship across the Pacific and translated the Bible and parts of the prayer book into Mandarin before he was elected bishop of Shanghai in 1877. Paralyzed by a stroke, he resigned his see in 1883 but over the next twenty years completed, with the help of his wife, a translation of the Bible into Wenli, typing some two thousand pages with the middle finger of his partially crippled hand. Four years before his death in 1906 he said, "I have sat in this chair for over twenty years. It seemed very hard at first. But God knew best. He kept me for the work for which I am best fitted."[9]

Cooperation and convergence characterize the continuing history of voluntary societies and centralized missionary structures in the Anglican Communion. The Church of England adopted the strategy of missionary bishops, one of whom was G. W. H. Knight-Bruce, the pioneer Anglican in Rhodesia whom we met in chapter three. Following the DFMS example, a Board of Missions was established in 1891 to provide a forum for the Church of England to share information about its missions abroad. Although the mission societies were not formally represented, many individuals working with them were members. On the American side, the Woman's Auxiliary to the Board of Missions was established by the 1871 General Convention, but it operated essentially as a voluntary society under the leadership of Mary Emery Twing and Julia Chester Emery. Its major role in mission funding continues today through the United Thank Offering coordinated by the auxiliary's successor organization, the Episcopal Church Women.

Adopting the ascendant corporation model of the business world, Episcopal centralization intensified with the establishment of the National Council in 1919, under which world mission was consolidated in a Department of Missions and Church Extension. Missiologist Ian Douglas has shown that as the United

States became an imperial power after the Spanish-American War and a global power after World War I, the Episcopal Church began to see its centralized self as "The National Church," with moral authority for bearing the American national ethos.[10] Following the lead of governmental interests abroad, the church initiated mission work in the Philippines, Cuba, Taiwan, and Latin America, diversifying to other parts of the world later in the century.

~ A Century of Self-Criticism

People exploring Christian mission in the twenty-first century can build on a rich legacy of reflection from the last century. Concerns that people today have about Christian mission were identified during the twentieth century most cogently by missionaries themselves and by Christians in the newer churches of the Global South. While expansion was the keynote of the nineteenth century, self-criticism was the mission movement's central theme during the twentieth century. Whether in evangelism or development, funding or leadership, cultural impact or interreligious relations, reassessing assumptions and goals was the order of the day in most churches and missionary-sending agencies.

Outlooks shifted radically between 1900 and 2000. "The evangelization of the world in this generation" was the vision of the Student Volunteer Movement that drew British and American young people into international mission in the century's early decades. Mission expansion was certainly the horizon of the influential World Missionary Conference held in Edinburgh in 1910. Meanwhile, missionaries themselves were suggesting receptive views of other religions, as we shall see in chapter five, and later in the century the "theology of religions" became a field of its own with important implications for mission.

The leadership strategy of western missions was questioned by Anglican China missionary Roland Allen in his pithy 1912 book *Missionary Methods: St. Paul's or Ours?* Whereas Paul would proclaim the gospel, gather a church, appoint leaders, and then move on, Allen observed missionaries giving lip service to self-government but postponing it indefinitely out of their own superiority complex and distrust of new converts.[11] Progress was made, however slowly, and at the 1928 Jerusalem conference of the International Missionary Council over fifty of the two hundred fifty delegates were members of the "younger churches" of the Global South. There S. C. Leung of China insisted that in newly evangelized areas missionaries must become part of the emerging church and not operate as a parallel authority competing with the indigenous church.

The growing maturity and mission power of churches in the Global South was world Christianity's principal development during the century. As early as 1903, the Indian Missionary Society was established by Anglicans in South India, and under the Church of South India today it has over one hundred missionaries serving across cultural and linguistic boundaries within India. Korean Christianity has become a major mission-sending force since the middle of the twentieth century. Explosive Christian growth in Africa has been fueled by indigenous mission vision, and people in the Global North have benefitted from the evangelistic travels of such leaders as the late Festo Kivengere, bishop of the Anglican Diocese of Kigezi in Uganda. In addition to becoming self-supporting, self-governing, and self-propagating, Christians in the Global South are increasingly "self-theologizing," exerting global influence through such figures as M. M. Thomas, Kwok Pui-lan, and Kosuke Koyama in Asia; Gustavo Guttiérez and Jon Sobrino in Latin America; and John Mbiti, John Pobee, Mercy Oduyoye, and Desmond Tutu in Africa. These and others have contributed to theological reflection in such areas as liberation, culture, poverty, feminism, globalization, and religious pluralism.

The Laymen's Foreign Missions Inquiry, sponsored for Asia by eight North American mission boards in the 1930s, critiqued not only global conversion goals but also the qualifications and theologies of missionaries. While affirming that Jesus manifested God uniquely, the commissioners called for collaboration with other religionists in creating "world understanding on a spiritual level." Secularism and materialism, not other religions, were the adversary, they said, anticipating a view common today. Controversy about the liberal tone of the Laymen's report set the stage for how the theological divide between fundamentalists and modernists in the 1920s would affect North American and British mission throughout the century. In the late 1920s, the approximately fourteen thousand non-Roman Catholic American missionaries came mostly from mainline churches such as Presbyterian, Methodist, Congregational, and Episcopal, with a sprinkling from independent mission groups. Late in the century, by contrast, most of the approximately thirty-five thousand non-Roman Catholic missionaries come from evangelical societies and churches, with just nine percent coming from groups associated with the World Council of Churches (WCC).[12]

Why this shift since mid-century? As ecumenical Christians sought to discern Christ's presence in other religions, they promoted dialogue and questioned evangelism and church-planting. Education, health, agriculture, and economic empowerment occupied many mission personnel, but then governments of newly independent nations began to address these concerns themselves. Solidarity with the liberation struggles of the oppressed became a major emphasis in ecumenical mission thinking, but it did not produce many missionary placements. As indigenous leaders took hold in the post-colonial era, missionaries often were no longer needed in pastoral and management roles, and in the early 1970s there was a short-lived call for a moratorium on sending missionaries.

Under these pressures, mainline churches down-sized their global outreach substantially. The number of Episcopal missionaries declined from an all-time high of 486 in 1933 to 263 in 1968, but the drop became precipitous when the church turned to address the racial and urban crises of America in the late 1960s. The General Convention Special Program allocated funds to the poor and oppressed in the United States, and budget cuts in the early 1970s reduced missionary appointments to about seventy. Meanwhile, Venture in Mission, the church-wide capital campaign of the mid-1970s, financed development and diocesan infrastructure projects around the world, expanding the Episcopal Church's role as a major source of money in the Anglican Communion. Venture reinstated the Volunteers for Mission program, which created a fresh flow of short-term, self-funded missioners as the numbers of fully funded mission appointees continued to decline.[13]

Meanwhile, with their evangelistic and church-planting emphases intact, conservative Protestant groups multiplied their missionaries and launched such global initiatives as the Lausanne Covenant for World Evangelization in 1974. Evangelicals initially resisted the justice emphasis of ecumenical gatherings like the World Council of Churches' 1968 Uppsala Assembly, because they saw evangelism getting lost in the shuffle. In recent years, however, they have incorporated justice into a holistic vision of mission.

∾ Organizational Diversity and Unity

As domestic priorities, financial constraints, and doubts about mission drastically reduced the Episcopal Church's global outreach in the early 1970s, many people in the pews remained committed to global engagement, especially those who were part of the evangelical renewal of the period. New mission initiatives were the fruit. In 1974, Alaska missionaries Walter and Louise Hannum founded the Episcopal Church Missionary Community to provide mission education and training, and today it organizes the triennial New Wineskins for Global Mission conference. On the British voluntary society model, the South American Missionary Society (SAMS) was founded in 1976 as a sister society of the British SAMS. From its first two missionaries sent to Arequipa, Peru, SAMS-USA has grown to more than fifty long-term missionaries and many short-term teams in Latin America and Spain who raise their own support from parishes, dioceses, and individuals. Episcopal World Mission (EWM) followed in 1982. Sharing of Ministries Abroad—its acronym SOMA recalls the Greek New Testament word for the *body* of Christ— was founded in 1985 as the American version of a British charismatic group "dedicated to fostering renewal in the Holy Spirit throughout the world." In the Anglican Church of Canada, a centralized mission program has been similarly complemented by the forming of groups such as SAMS-Canada.

The blooming of new and autonomous initiatives in world mission renewed the vision of many Episcopalians. Others found it confusing and disturbing. How would new efforts relate to the central structure of the Domestic and Foreign Missionary Society (DFMS)? Could parishes and dioceses support both the new organizations and the traditional avenues of mission? Who were the "official missionaries" of the church? Amid the possibilities for misunderstanding and competition, a series of world mission conferences sponsored between 1980 and 1988 by several mission agencies and the University of the South in Sewanee, Tennessee, prepared the way for the Episcopal Council for Global Mission (ECGM), founded in 1990. ECGM brought together voluntary societies, DFMS agencies, parishes, and dioceses to support one another and collaborate as a network in promoting world mission throughout the church.

The Episcopal Partnership for Global Mission (EPGM) replaced ECGM in 2000 as a way to bring the networking among mission groups into a recognized relationship with General Convention. Executive Council's recognition of the missionaries of all member organizations overcomes the previous problematic distinction between "official" Episcopal missionaries and "other" Episcopal missionaries. On behalf of the entire church, EPGM embraces and promotes the rich diversity of mission visions within the church, as one organization might focus on starting new congregations, for instance, while another focuses on economic empowerment. EPGM offers a model of groups partnering for mission in the midst of differences about other issues in the church's life, such as homosexuality. The network makes it easier for both international partners and ordinary Episcopalians to envision the church's global outreach and to relate to particular organizations within that outreach. The organizations anticipate that the partnership will release more energy, personnel, and funding to enable all Episcopalians to participate in God's mission.

In the Anglican Church of Canada, the Partners in Mission Committee of General Synod has sought to bring greater unity to Canadian world mission while affirming the independence of newly formed voluntary societies. The Church of England has moved over the last century toward partnership among its voluntary societies, each with a longstanding heritage of autonomy. In 1921 the Overseas Committee of the (newly formed) Church Assembly included formal representatives of the societies. The Partnership for World Mission (PWM), established in 1978, provided an official forum for the Church of England's eleven major world mission agencies to relate to the General Synod formed in 1970, and in 1991 PWM became a constituent committee of the Synod's Board of Mission. Thus on both sides of the Atlantic, Anglicans have been able both to affirm diverse views of world mission and to establish structures that enable groups to work together.

∾ From Paternalism to Partnership

The growth of the Anglican Communion in the twentieth century called on Anglicans to recast their vision of mission. As new nations and new Anglican provinces were born with the breakup of colonialism, relationships between churches of the Global North and churches of the Global South needed to transcend the paternalism and dependency of the past. "Mutual Responsibility and Interdependence in the Body of Christ" (MRI) was the vision of the Anglican Congress of 1963 in Toronto:

> The keynotes of our time are equality, interde-
> pendence, mutual responsibility.... Our unity
> in Christ, expressed in our full communion, is
> the most profound bond among us, in all our
> political and racial and economic diversi-
> ty.... Mission is not kindness of the lucky to the
> unlucky; it is mutual, united obedience to the
> one God whose mission it is. The form of the
> Church must reflect that.... In substance, what
> we are really asking for is the rebirth of the
> Anglican Communion, which means the death
> of many old things but—infinitely more—the
> birth of entirely new relationships.[14]

Ironically, the MRI initiative soon focused on a
"Directory of Projects" that churches in the Global
North were to fund in a traditional one-directional
way. As a concept, however, MRI continues to express
Anglicans' longing for mature and mutual relationships across the divisions created by geography,
money, race, class, power, and history.

Crucial over the past thirty years has been the concept of partnership in mission that the Anglican
Consultative Council put forward as a guiding principle in 1973:

> The emergence everywhere of autonomous
> churches in independent nations has challenged
> our inherited idea of mission as a movement
> from "Christendom" in the West to the "non-
> Christian" world. In its place has come the con-
> viction that there is but one mission in all the
> world, and that this one mission is shared by
> the world-wide Christian community. The
> responsibility for mission in any place belongs
> *primarily* to the church in that place. However,
> the universality of the gospel and the oneness of

God's mission mean also that this mission must be shared in each and every place with fellow-Christians from each and every part of the world with their distinctive insights and contributions. If we once acted as though there were only givers who had nothing to receive and receivers who had nothing to give, the oneness of the missionary task must make us all both givers and receivers.[15]

Here Anglicans rejected the superiority and inferiority complexes of the colonial past. Mission does not necessarily entail imperialism, for the missionary recognizes that his or her home place is equally a mission field, and every context needs the insights of Christians from other places. Thus as missionaries go out from Chicago or London to Brazil or Malaysia, they will also welcome missionaries from São Paulo or Kuala Lumpur who may have particular gifts to offer in America or Britain. Partnership consists in Christians joining their visions, efforts, and resources to carry out God's mission, whether at home or in their fellow Christians' home places.

As Anglican partners embraced free-flowing mutuality they released new energy for mission. Implementing the concept had a programmatic component as each autonomous Anglican church, called a province, was encouraged to hold a Partnership in Mission (PIM) Consultation with Anglicans from other provinces to help it discern and carry out God's mission. A number of such consultations were held in provinces around the world, both north and south, during the 1970s and 80s before they petered out in the 90s.

As a concept, partnership is probably the single most cited criterion of mission effectiveness as missionaries assess their own work and as mission agencies shape their strategies. The Church Mission Society in Britain incorporated partnership so organically into its ethos that it calls its personnel "mission partners" not "missionaries," and the building in London that houses CMS, the United Society for the Propagation of the Gospel, and several other agencies was named Partnership House. Individuals and organizations have experienced the partnership model as a standing invitation to relationship and a useful guard against neo-colonial and "Lone Ranger" ways of doing mission.

⁓ History's Lessons
How can we learn from the history of Christian mission? Resisting quick generalizations is one key as we look carefully at individuals, incidents, and particular developments. Being willing to live with the ambiguity of real life rather than insisting on the crystal clarity of our ideals is another. Developing an incarnational perspective on the life of the church is foundational. As God took flesh in the human being Jesus, so also the continuing presence of Christ in the church is incarnational, affected by humanity as well as inspired by God. "We have this treasure in *earthen* vessels," wrote St. Paul. In those vessels, we also have a *treasure!*

E. Stanley Jones was an American Methodist evangelist in India from 1910 to 1970 and also a friend of Mahatma Gandhi. Troubled by Gandhi's tactic of fasting for days in order to gain concessions from the British authorities, he asked Gandhi, "Isn't your fasting a species of coercion?" Gandhi replied slowly, "Yes, the same kind of coercion which Jesus exercises upon you from the cross."[16] Gandhi was not a Christian, but he learned deeply from Christian proclamation.

Gandhi also had advice for Christian mission. Jones tells the story:

> In conversation with him one day I said, "Mahatma Gandhi, I am very anxious to see Christianity naturalised in India, so that it shall be no longer a foreign thing identified with a foreign people and a foreign government, but a part of the national life of India and contributing its power to India's uplift and redemption. What would you suggest that we do to make that possible?" He very gravely and thoughtfully replied: "I would suggest, first, that all of you Christians, missionaries and all, must begin to live more like Jesus Christ. Second, I would suggest that you must practice your religion without adulterating or toning it down. Third, I would suggest that you must put your emphasis upon love, for love is the centre and soul of Christianity. Fourth, I would suggest that you study the non-Christian religions and culture more sympathetically in order to find the good that is in them, so that you might have a more sympathetic approach to the people."[17]

This is advice most Christians would affirm. This is also advice from a non-Christian who sought not to end Christian mission but to reform it.

Chapter Five

Christian Mission and Other Religions

One of the most beautiful services of evening prayer I have witnessed was by the Ganges River in Banaras, the holiest city of the Hindus and the oldest continuously inhabited city in the world. Wide stone stairways, called *ghats*, descend into the river, and on either side ancient temples crowd over the water as if about to jump in. Over the centuries the Ganges has changed course and some temples are partly submerged, becoming architectural images of the immersion that millions of Hindu pilgrims undertake in the river as they seek holiness and communion with the divine.

At the central Dashashvamedh Ghat thousands of people come each day to do their *dharshan*, or devotion, through meditating and bathing. On this particular afternoon, a Brahman priest was publicly reciting a portion of the *Mahabharata*, the great epic poem of conflict and redemption. The several-hour reading was interspersed with chants that the gathered devotees repeated after the priest until the deafening beat of a drum brought the recitation to a close.

The *Ganga puja*, or Ganges prayer, was offered at sunset. Incense was lit, and a brass pot of Ganga water was passed around a burning lamp. As they sang devotional songs in Hindi, worshipers purchased lotus leaf boats, each with a flower and a small clay oil lamp, called a *dipa*. Lighting the little wick, the worshiper then placed the boat in the river, where it slowly floated away. I bought one, put it in the water, and watched it join the crowd of lamps moving down the river in the dusk. What did that signify for me? Prayer, certainly, and a sense that my personal pilgrimage in God was joining that of others.

I had gone to Banaras as a young adult to look and to listen and found myself drawn into contemplation. Dressed in north Indian *pajama* and *kurta*, I sat for hours on the *ghats*, just being there. It was a life period not of searching exactly, but of exploring my own religious heritage. Being in Banaras was a way of bonding with the spirituality that had surrounded me while growing up. In touch with Christian roots as well, I had been singing in my university's church choir and had recently taken a course in the work of twentieth-century theologians like Karl Barth, Paul Tillich, and Hans Küng.

During those days of sitting by the river, I struck up an acquaintance with a diesel engine designer named Rangaswamy, a Banaras resident who came daily to the river to meditate. He told me about how the Sanskrit scriptures developed and how each sub-caste of the Brahmans is associated with one of the four Vedas. Rangaswamy had little use for the ritual aspect of Hindu worship, though, and he considered the riverside priests to be ignorant impostors. Sure enough, when pressed, the priest on one particular day could not recite even one *mantra* and spent most of his time haggling with devotees over the prices of blessings. I suggested that ritual could still be a guide, a discipline for nurturing the soul. No, said

Rangaswamy, *puja* (prayer) was for him an inner attitude of concentration, for which ritual was useless, and he devoted his life to *karma*, which he defined as right action.

Rangaswamy taught me a Sanskrit *mantra*, and I used it. "I am beginning to feel," I wrote in my journal, "some of that compelling force which is essential to religion, in the sense that I am becoming unable to do without the exercise of inner meditation, that inletting of peace, a calm supremely satisfying which I have come to know." I bathed in the river. Stilled in the presence of death, I spent time at the burning *ghat*, where people bring their dead to be cremated, after which the ashes are poured into the sacred waters. India's poverty was everywhere apparent, especially in the narrow winding lanes that lead to the *ghats*, for there sat the maimed, the lame, and the blind begging coins from all of us on our way to commune with the divine.

Much later, but still as a young adult, I renewed my Christian commitment. With long and receptive exposure to other religions, why didn't I become, say, a Hindu? After all, one of my American schoolmates from India became a Baha'i, and another is now a Buddhist. Beyond my own story, that query suggests the kinds of questions people have about world religions and mission today.

∿ Why Christianity?

The presence of various religions side by side, not only in the Two-Thirds World but also in the Global North, prompts both Christians and non-Christians to question the mission impulse. The simplest question asked is something like, "Why try to convert people who already have their own religion?" Those who understand that conversion need not involve anyone "trying"~to make~something~happen for someone else may yet ask, "What basis is there for supposing that Christianity is a fuller or more valid way than other religions?" People aware of weaknesses in various religious groups ask, "Sure, you can point to problems among Buddhists or Muslims or whomever, but how do you explain the fact that there are just as many problems among Christians?" Those who know people who practice other faiths may ask, "We have some Sikh neighbors who are just as spiritually centered and ethically good as any Christians we know, so why urge them to consider Christianity?" And people who have actually explored another religion may ask, "I happen to be a Christian, but I've learned a lot from Buddhism, so why would I suggest that a Buddhist become a Christian?"

These questions can also be asked in more abstract ways. In religion, why choose one way over another? If one does choose a particular spiritual path, does that choice signify anything beyond personal inclination or the influence of one's family or cultural background? Is there "truth value" to religion beyond the validity of a purely personal fulfillment in one's religious practice? Assuming there is a God, isn't it possible that all the religions are equally valid ways of experiencing God? If so, what grounds are there for any particular projection of Christian identity and life among non-Christians? As I led a class of inquirers interested in being confirmed in the Episcopal Church, theological and historical discussions over several sessions drifted repeatedly into the issue of the status of other religions. Finally one class member observed, "The question we seem to be asking is not, Why Anglicanism? but, Why Christianity?"

At the opening of the twenty-first century, religion is as important to people in most parts of the world as it ever was, and, if religious strife is a measure of religious passion, religion today may be more important than ever. This is an ironic counterpoint to the slow demise of religion predicted early in the twentieth century, when many thought faith would crumble under the pressures of Marxist politics, Freudian psychology, and consumer society. Instead, the late twentieth century alone saw such developments as the reemergence of Christian communities in China; the establishment of a Shiite Muslim state in Iran; the rise of nationalist Hinduism in India; a global resurgence of Christian pentecostalism; mutual terror between Protestants and Roman Catholics in Northern Ireland; and strife between Christians and Muslims in Sudan, Nigeria, and Indonesia. Although religious conflicts have geopolitical dimensions, they are not reducible simply to economics and politics, for religious convictions play a strong role in them.

Christian mission is often regarded as pouring oil on the flames of religious conflict. In India, for instance, Pope John Paul II's 1999 call for Asian Catholics to "penetrate the hearts of Asian peoples" was depicted by Hindu leaders as a Christian effort to divide India for motives of greed and ambition. The Southern Baptist Convention's successive "targeting" of Muslims, Hindus, and Jews in its evangelistic campaigns in the United States upset not only those groups but also Christian churches that felt this approach lacked respect for non-Christian religions. Mission work by any religious group is prohibited in China, and mission by any non-Muslim group is prohibited in such nations as Iran, Saudi Arabia, and Pakistan. To the extent that Christian mission stimulates changes in religious affiliation, mission does break up the religious unity of a particular part of the world. If that happens in a context of negative advertising about the alternatives, mission can be seen as promoting destructive competition among religions.

In this environment of tension and debate, we see that Christian mission's relationship to other religions bears on personal spirituality and community life, on classic theological questions, and on ideals of world harmony and peace. The issue is especially acute because Christianity is the world's most populous religion. The Christian stance toward other religions will affect more people than, say, the Baha'i, Parsi, or Shinto stance toward other religions.

～ Attitudes of Christian Missionaries

One stereotype of Christian missionaries is that throughout history they have condemned other faiths as having nothing to offer and have sought to convert people to a religion identical to their own. In fact, mission history exhibits a wide diversity of approaches. In our historical review, we have seen how the New Testament both asserts the centrality of Christ and looks for points of contact with other religions. We have seen early Christianity's rapid growth amid many religious options and Justin Martyr's search for a relationship with Greek philosophy. We have witnessed Christendom's use of coercion and the disaster of the Crusades. We have heard Pope Gregory urge the adaptation of pagan temples and seen Jesuits seeking to present the gospel in the religious idioms of China and India. We have heard Anglican evangelical Henry Venn anticipate that the Christianity of new converts will differ from that of the missionaries. In the flood-tide of European imperialism we have heard high churchman G. W. H. Knight-Bruce conclude that the Shona had no religion at all before the advent of Christianity. And that is just a small sampling of the diversity!

Supporters of European and American mission in the nineteenth century often based their enthusiasm on a dismissal of other religions. A fairly typical Anglican assessment of Asian religions is found in an 1877 letter from William Bacon Stevens, bishop of Pennsylvania, supporting Samuel Isaac Joseph Schereschewsky's plan to establish a Christian college in China:

> [The Chinese] have all the elements of modern civilization except the one important factor of Christianity. Their several religions, however philosophical they may be in some of their aspects, are but masked forms of idolatry and pantheism. . . . Buddhism and Taoism and Confucianism, the three religious sects of the Chinese, are interwoven throughout with false history, false science, false geography, false chronology, false philosophy, yet all these falsities alleging some divine basis; thus making a false theology uphold a defective education, and a defective education upholds a false religion.[1]

Actual experience of other religions often makes a difference, and in the late 1800s the views of missionaries on the ground began to include more appreciation and generosity. Missionaries left home thinking that other religions had nothing to offer, but in the field many began to feel God had been at work there, even as they believed Christ was central. An especially telling example of this is the responses missionaries made to a questionnaire sent out in preparation for the 1910 World Missionary Conference in Edinburgh by the conference's Commission on the Missionary Message in Relation to Non-Christian Religions. One of the questions was, "What attitude should the Christian preacher take towards the religion of the people among whom he labours?" Scholar Kenneth Cracknell has found that 145 of the 160 responses emphasized "sympathy, respect, and appreciation." For instance, a Church Missionary Society missionary in the Punjab wrote, "Our attitude should be one of the greatest sympathy." A Lutheran missionary in Madras recommended "deep and genuine sympathy." Some respondents expressed reservations about Islam, but from Rawalpindi, now part of Pakistan, a woman missionary with the Society for the Propagation of the Gospel in Foreign Parts wrote, "We have to find out what is good in their religions. . . . For the foreign missionary especially, the teaching should be rather constructive than destructive." An Episcopal missionary in Shanghai highlighted "an attitude of understanding and sympathy." An SPG missionary in Burma wrote, "The missionary should rejoice in every element of truth and goodness that he finds in the religion and the practice of the people with whom he has to deal."

When asked about points of contacts, the missionaries cited elements they could build on in other religions, including links with African religions, at the time often termed animistic. Thomas Slater, a well-known London Missionary Society member, compared the *Brahman*, or divine essence, of Hindu thought with the *Logos*, or divine Word, that Christian thought has identified with Christ. Pointing to Jesus' statement about the law and the prophets, "I have not come to abolish but to fulfill" (Matthew 5:17), many respondents saw Christianity as completing, fulfilling, or transfiguring the partial revelations found in other religions.

"Has your experience in missionary labour," the missionaries were asked, "altered in either form or substance your impression as to what constitute the most important and vital elements in the Christian

Gospel?" Many readily acknowledged that their work *had* affected their views and recommended modifications in western versions of Christianity. Some had gone out with a Latin theology of strict categories, but in their work they developed a Greek theology that was more cosmic and inclusive in its vision of God's presence and revelation in the world.[2] Missionaries found support for their evolving views in the work of such theologians as Frederick Denison Maurice, a British Anglican. In his 1845 lectures *The Religions of the World and their Relations to Christianity*, Maurice declared there must be light in other religions or they could not persist, and he suggested that Christ is at work in other religions and cultures.[3] Thus contact with other religions, the primary object of mission labor, changed missionaries' views of both those religions and the Christianity with which they went.

Living this dynamic in the second half of the twentieth century were Murray and Mary Rogers, who went to India in 1946 as CMS missionaries. They served their first term at the Allahabad Agricultural Institute, a mission compound where, Murray told me, "the cross was talked about but was not much in evidence." They spent time at Sevagram, the *ashram* established by Gandhi, where they were among six Christians in a community of three hundred people worshiping and serving together. At Sevagram "the cross was not talked about, but it was very much there." After a year with a Hindu family, the Rogers in 1954 began living with a few other Christians near Bareilly in north India. In time, their place and group came to be called an *ashram*, which in Hindu tradition is a small community of prayer and learning that gathers spontaneously around a *guru*, or spiritual teacher. No one claimed to be *guru*, but Murray functioned as one, and the community was named Jyotiniketan, Community of Light.

The vision was to live as a Christian presence through the worship patterns and thought forms of Hinduism. The Rogers wore saffron robes and with their companions developed a liturgical life that included Sanskrit hymns that both drew on Hindu contemplation and anchored the worship deeply in Christ. Eucharist was celebrated daily at dawn after silent meditation, and the noonday and evening offices highlighted intercessions focused on global justice and peace. Community members developed friendships in the villages, offered hospitality to locals and travelers, and ran a small dispensary. Jyotiniketan was never intentionally evangelistic, but the Rogers saw their life as Christian witness, and the whole enterprise had a profound effect on me as an eighteen-year-old.

When in 1958 the Rogers discontinued their connection with the CMS, the local district commissioner wanted to know why they did not appear on the role of registered missionaries. For him, a missionary was someone who took orders from abroad, received money from outside the country, and tried to persuade people to change their religion and become Christians. Explaining that none of those criteria applied to them, the Rogers said, "We live here to try to deepen our love for God and for other people." The commissioner recommended that their visa status be changed to "spiritual devotees," for, he said, "It is transparently clear that if you are a spiritual devotee you cannot be a missionary." It was done, but the comment indicated the tragically de-spiritualized impression of Christianity conveyed by generations of missionaries busy with their institutions.

In subsequent moves, the Rogers lived out the vision of Jyotiniketan in Jerusalem, Hong Kong, and Ontario, learning through the end of the century from Judaism, Islam, Buddhism, Taoism, Shintoism, and Amerindian religion. What is remarkable about the Rogers is not so much that as Christians they explored other religions, but that with such deep engagement with the range of global religious experience they were yet so profoundly centered in Christ. They avoided conventional trappings of the missionary role, but the Christian witness they offered in a life-long encounter with the other fulfilled an important dimension of God's mission.

∾ Encounter with Other Religions

Many Christians experience the gospel's relation to people of other faiths as a major quandary, both as they sort out their theology of religions and as they seek closer cooperation with those who have a different religious orientation. My purpose here is not so much to advocate a particular stance as to shed light on how one might go about clarifying one's stance.

Incarnational expectancy is a life orientation that can midwife us through the birth canal of interreligious encounter and understanding. Jesus' proclamation of the kingdom of God articulated his confidence that *God was up to something in the world*, something decisive, and that he himself had a crucial part in it. That is still true. It is true of God, it is true of the world, and it is true of us. God calls us to engage the world expecting to glimpse something of what God is doing and how we can participate. That is as true of our encounter with other religions as it is of our encounter with anything else. "Sincere reverence" toward those religions is how the Second Vatican

Council put it. God may be up to something, and we need the eyes and ears to see and hear it.

The expectancy is incarnational in the sense that interreligious encounters are not encounters with other *religions* but with other *people*. Reading the Koran or the Bhagavad Gita can help, but what if a religious tradition has no written scripture, as I found with *Chivanhu*, the ancient religion *"of the people"* in Zimbabwe? It is living and breathing people who communicate and incarnate what a particular faith truly is. Clarifying one's interreligious stance needs to be a relational enterprise in which we plunge into actual encounters with other people, eager to listen, discover, and share. Those encounters help us build our theology, whereas beginning with the theological puzzles may leave us just puzzled! In planning a forum series on Islam at St. Peter's in Cambridge, we scheduled parishioners to research various aspects of Islam, but invited the nearby Boston Islamic Society to send a presenter for the first week. Well, the Muslims were so enthusiastic that they brought seven people, who then returned for several weeks and for the last session invited us to their mosque for a service and discussion. A forum supposedly *about* Islam ended up being an experience *with* Muslims, and it was memorable.

Incarnational expectancy also means that we are eager for what God may be doing in and through ourselves. An interreligious encounter is a full encounter only if all participants share their sense of the divine. As you wish to hear the fullness of another's religious experience, you can usually be confident that the other is eager to hear yours as well. This is witness of the most basic sort, and, for Christians, testifying has always been a natural fruit of experiencing the triune God. You owe it to the dialogue to be transparent about what God is doing with you. Witness and dialogue are companions, not adversaries, for witness stimulates dialogue, and dialogue both shapes and depends on witness.

Every Christian's stance toward other religions is likely the fruit of unique experiences and reflections, but three general positions can be identified: exclusivism, inclusivism, and pluralism. An exclusivist believes salvation, often conceptualized as eternal community with God, is available only through an explicitly acknowledged relationship with Christ. The exclusivist views other religions as having little or nothing to offer and their devotees as mistaken or deceived. Christianity is affirmed as unique, definitive, absolute, normative, and superior in relation to other religions.

An inclusivist affirms both the spiritual richness of other faiths and the centrality of Christ, believing that Christ is the source of the truth and communion available in other religions and that they find their true fulfillment in Christ. The most illustrative phrase coming from this position has been "the unknown Christ of Hinduism," which expressed Raimundo Panikkar's view that "recognizing the presence of *God* in other religions is equivalent to proclaiming the presence of Christ in them, 'for in him all things subsist.'"[4]

Pluralism, the third position, is the principal challenge many Christians wrestle with today. A pluralist believes that other religions have their own autonomous validity, independent of Christ, that God works through them as fully as God works through Christianity; we Christians have as much to learn from them as they do from us. A pluralist is likely to argue that faith should be God-centered, or theocentric, rather than Christ-centered, or Christocentric. Some pluralists see all religions as different ways of experiencing the same ultimate reality, as in different views of one mountain, and they look for shared themes among religions. Other pluralists, wary of homogenizing distinct visions, insist on the uniqueness of each religion and are unsure whether or how religions can relate to one another. Rejecting claims of superiority as religious imperialism, pluralists tend to see any religion as a human, historical construction that cannot be absolute in its claims. Religious experience is too vast to be contained by any one religion, they believe, and human suffering demands that all religions work together against poverty, disease, injustice, violence, and environmental degradation.

In the midst of these options and perhaps transcending them, "witness" is a pivotal term for our reflection. When Jesus sent his friends out, he said, "You shall be my witnesses." We all see thousands of events and objects every day, but we use the term "witness" for someone who has seen something so important that it is equally important that they testify to what they have seen, as at a roadside accident or in a courtroom. The word for a witness in the Greek New Testament is *martus*, from which our word "martyr" is derived. The martyrs depicted at Westminster Abbey, for instance, considered what they had seen in Christ so crucial that they were willing to die rather than repress their testimony. The approach of Christians to people of other faiths, the 1998 Lambeth Conference said, should be marked by openness, cooperation, exploration, listening, and also "sharing and witnessing to all we know of the good news of Christ as our debt of love to all people whatever their religious affiliation."[5]

Living with other religions becomes a quandary for Christian mission only when mission is understood, as it so often is, simply as "trying to convert other people." The first fruit of Christian experience is neither a condemnation of other religions nor a conversion campaign but joyful and natural witness to the presence of the triune God in one's life. Returning to my own story, I have learned much from the spiritual richness of religions in Asia and Africa. Yet I rejoice in the conviction that in Christ Jesus God has enacted a turning point in universal history, and this conviction arose from the existential experience of Christ coming to me. Amid all the other options, what do I find compelling about the gospel? The proclamation that God works within history, as well as beyond history engages the complexity of existence as I experience it. God's incarnation in Christ expresses God's commitment to humanity more "riskingly" and comprehensively than any other act of God I have heard of. Jesus himself is a magnetic figure in vision and spirituality, compassion, and courage. The cross engages profoundly the alienation and brokenness of humanity. The resurrection offers to the vast universe an embracing hope of re-creation. I could go on, but that, in brief, is what I witness to in mission.

The validity of Christian mission does not depend on what one concludes about the validity of other religions, nor on what one believes about the eternal destiny of people who are not Christians. In fact, today among the missionaries of any of the historic western churches—such as Anglican, Lutheran, Baptist, Roman Catholic, Methodist, Congregational, Presbyterian, or Mennonite—one will find exclusivists, inclusivists, and pluralists. In any of these stances, sheer and simple witness is still intrinsic to Christian faith, and it is the heart of all mission. Said the World Council of Churches in 1989, "We cannot point to any other way of salvation than Jesus Christ; at the same time we cannot set limits to the saving power of God."[6] In this sense, witness is equivalent to mission, and there are as many kinds of witness as there are kinds of mission. Exactly what our witness accomplishes is not something we can control. It is sufficient that Christian witness enters the many-voiced religious conversation of today's world, so like the world of the first century. Conversion, learning, healing, justice—any of these things may happen through Christian witness in that conversation, but that is God's business, just as people's eternal destiny is in God's hands, not ours. Our trust is that the Holy Spirit will do with our witness just as the Holy Spirit chooses. Now, as at the beginning, the mission is not ours but God's.

～ Mission and the Ecumenical Struggle

Related to our stance toward other religions is the question of unity and disunity in mission among the churches. One major concern about modern Christian mission is the exportation of denominationalism from the Global North to the Global South. The multiplicity of Christian denominations around the world reflects how energetically the northern churches have projected themselves outward in world mission since the eighteenth century. People in other parts of the world have often simply found themselves to be members of the denomination through which they became Christian. Some have felt pressed to choose among competing church affiliations—Roman Catholic, Presbyterian, Anglican—with all their imported varieties of worship, theology, and polity.

The resulting disunity is one of the strongest reproaches lodged against the mission efforts of Christian churches, and with good reason. "That they all may be one" was Jesus' prayer for his followers, doubtless for their own sake, but also for the sake of the gospel being credible in the world: "As you, Father, are in me and I am in you, may they also be in us, *so that the world may believe that you have sent me"* (John 17:21). Since unity is vital to the appeal and authenticity of mission, we Christians have long known that our disunity is a scandal that cripples our witness in the world.

An early ecumenical impulse to resist the denominational fracturing of mission was the founding of the London Missionary Society (LMS), a joint venture by Congregationalists, Anglicans, Presbyterians, and Wesleyans, in 1796. They were resolved that no particular denomination would be preached and that issues of church government would be left to new converts to arrange on their own. In time, however, denominational concerns prompted participating churches to go their own way, and the LMS became a Congregationalist venture. The twentieth century saw the founding of numerous voluntary societies that were ecumenical in the sense of welcoming missionaries from diverse churches. Many of these groups, however, espouse evangelical or fundamentalist approaches so distinctive that their impact has been essentially denominational among the peoples who receive them. In heavily missionized areas like Papua New Guinea, some groups have grown not mainly through conversions of non-Christians but through intentionally drawing people away from other churches.

In the Chicago-Lambeth Quadrilateral of 1886 and 1888 Anglicans expressed openness to church union and invited other churches' consideration on the basis of what they believed were four fundamentals of the early and undivided church: Scripture as "containing all things necessary to salvation"; the Apostles' and Nicene Creeds, the latter as "the sufficient statement of the Christian faith"; the sacraments of baptism and

eucharist) and "the Historic Episcopate, locally adapted in the methods of its administration to the varying
needs of the nations and peoples called of God into the
unity of His Church" (BCP 876–878). The social reality that our sense of church identity resides as much in
ethos as it does in theology may partly account for
why the Quadrilateral's adequate but minimal definition of Christianity has failed to generate ecumenical
enthusiasm. Practically, Anglican interpretations of
the historic episcopate stalled initially promising discussions with Methodists in Britain and with the
Consultation on Church Union (now the Churches of
Christ Uniting) in the United States.

In the 1850s, mission societies and churches began
gathering in conferences to deepen ecumenical understanding as a basis for greater cooperation in mission.
The most influential of these was the 1910 World
Missionary Conference in Edinburgh, where the
organizers deliberately set aside issues of doctrine and
polity to concentrate on mission strategy. By implementing a crucial intuition that mission is an avenue
of Christian unity, they prompted the establishment
of not only the International Missionary Council but
also the Life and Work movement and the Faith and
Order movement, out of which grew the World
Council of Churches in 1948.

In founding the united churches of South India,
North India, Pakistan, and Bangladesh, from 1947 on,
Christians in southern Asia were saying, in effect,
"While we became Christians through the work of
many different churches, we will not be imprisoned
by the denominationalism of the Global North. As
heirs of Anglican, Methodist, Presbyterian, Reformed,
Congregational, and Lutheran influences, we choose,
instead, to develop a form of church life that will continue to unite Christians in the future." Meanwhile,

however, denominations continue to multiply around the world, from 1,880 in 1900 to 33,800 in 2000![7] A common African response to perceived weaknesses in the church life suggested by missionaries has been not to unite inherited groups but to found entirely new churches, so that in sub-Saharan Africa there are now over eight thousand church traditions founded by Africans, the vast majority during the twentieth century. As we saw with the Marange Apostles, many of these groups are scarcely ecumenical in spirit, and they can be just as critical of other African-initiated churches as they are of mission-founded churches. Distinct Christian groupings are also proliferating in other parts of the world, such as China and Korea.

Is such division simply a behavior learned from the division-prone Christians of the north? Partly, but not entirely. The missionary movement's stress on scripture translation democratizes religious initiative, so that the central source of authority, the Bible, becomes accessible to anyone to read and interpret in his or her own language. As the Gambian missiologist Lamin Sanneh points out, once the Bible is translated, initiative and authority pass decisively from the missioner to the missionized, regardless of how the missioner may seek to retain control.[8] Scripture translation asserts implicitly that any language and, by extension, any culture is a worthy vehicle of God's revelation in Christ. Far from being an innocuous preliminary in mission work, translating what an indigenous people may in time regard as God's word into their language and conceptual framework catalyzes new and powerful thinking by them about their culture, the gospel, and God. Among newly evangelized peoples, this process often and inevitably produces new and distinct church traditions and institutions.

At this juncture in history, the genie of church diversity is out of the bottle, and pressing for organic unity among churches may be futile, whether at home or abroad. The key to addressing our disunity is simply an ecumenical spirit—affirming one another's faith in Christ, prizing that unity as more important than the differences that divide us, learning what is distinctive about each other, and resolving to cooperate in practical mission. That sounds like a chiché until one encounters the opposite. While teaching at an Anglican seminary in Africa, I was taken aback by the students' skeptical questions about the major African-initiated churches in their own country: "These new churches, do you think they are real churches? And these people, should we see them as real Christians?" Surprised at my own passion, I urged them to realize that these are not abstract theological and ecclesiological questions. Rather, how the students regard other churches that call themselves Christian is crucial to their future ministries and to the mission of Anglicanism in Africa. When Anglicans—or Lutherans or Baptists or any Christians—censor other churches as non-Christian, we isolate ourselves and distort the witness we could offer together. As we accept other Christian groups, in all their diversity, as fellow pilgrims in Christ, we learn how the gospel is taking root in particular cultures and ready ourselves to form partnerships in the one mission of God in the world.

Chapter Six

Mission in Many Cultures

Shona names or English names? That common question in Zimbabwe highlights the complexities in mission's relation to the many cultures of the world. Among Shona people, the family name is always Shona, but the early missionaries encouraged new converts to give their children *Christian* names, so many were given biblical names like Esther and John, Miriam and Peter, Elizabeth and Lazarus. But other names cropped up, too, like Stanley and Mildred, Robert and Emily, Rose and William. Whether by missionary suggestion or indigenous inference, many came to prefer such names over Shona names. Why? They were *English* names, picked up from missionary families, imitated from colonial officials, or gleaned from English literature and history.

Many Shona people today grieve their parents' preference for English names, but they understand what happened. The impact of English-speaking culture, when linked to the economic and political triumph of British colonial power, undermined Shona people's confidence in their own culture, including their own language. Black Zimbabweans today are grateful for the enormous contribution made by mission education, but they do not appreciate how their parents sometimes were not allowed to speak their mother tongue in school. With their own children, many are consciously reappropriating their Shona heritage. For instance, Mildred and Daniel Mbwando, personal friends, gave Shona names to their six daughters: Nyasha, Rutendo, Zvinaiye, Mazviita, Tanyaradzwa, and Vimbainashe, which mean, respectively, Grace, Faith, Thank you (to God), It's-Up-To-Him (God), Hope-in-the-Lord, and We-Have-Been-Comforted. What could be more Christian?!

The names issue is just one among many that prompt concern about mission and culture. The popular 1986 film *The Mission* depicts movingly how South American Indian converts were caught between the eighteenth-century territorial claims of Spain and Portugal and how Jesuit missionaries tried in vain to protect them. I could not help wondering, though: Why were the Indians' musical skills turned to playing and making violins for the courts of Europe instead of to their own musical heritage? Victorian-era missionaries were embarrassed by nakedness, so they set to work clothing the people they found in Latin America and Africa. Customary practices in marriage, child nurture, and household organization felt the impact of missionary critique and innovation. In line with denominational loyalties, church life was organized according to the patterns of western churches. Western liturgies were translated into indigenous languages for local use, as were hymnals, often with the lyrics set in meters matching the original tunes in, say, England, Germany, or the United States. Church architecture mimicked buildings in the sending countries, and congregational organization reproduced the presbyteries, conferences, or dioceses of the sending churches. As we have seen among the

Jesuits, for instance, and with the Rogers in India, the history is by no means entirely negative, but clearly a good deal of mission work was carried out on the assumption that West is best.

This legacy has vaulted cultural concern up to a place beside interreligious concern in the modern debates about Christian mission. Respect for other religions and respect for other cultures—these are the two most urgent questions for mission today. If witness is indeed a natural fruit of Christian faith (the interreligious issue), how can that witness be offered across ethnic and national boundaries without violating the culture of the people to whom the missionary goes? Many people are dismayed by the erosion of tribal, ethnic, and national cultures around the world through the importation of modern western culture. In the 1930s some foresaw the emergence of a "world culture" that would be more humane and make cultural distinctions less important. Today, the world's best-known expression is "Okay!", the most widely known name is Coca-Cola, and we grieve the effects of Euro-American market culture around the world. Thoughtful people now value, at least theoretically, any and every human culture and realize that the erosion of culture involves to some degree the destruction of a people's identity. With mission's legacy of undermining cultures, many Christians are understandably cautious about involving themselves in a cross-cultural venture that is also Christian.

～ Cultural Chauvinism and Mission

Where do negative views about other cultures come from? At the most basic level, they probably arise from a fundamental human tendency to see one's own group as the main group, the most worthwhile group, the best group. Other groups are therefore viewed as peripheral, less worthwhile, not as good. One of the Native American groups in Canada carried this distinction so far that in their language the word for "human" was reserved only for members of their group, and did not apply to other people. Group chauvinism is doubtless a defensive extension of personal egoism: if my group is the best, it deserves to win in any contest where my personal well-being is at stake. Xenophobia, the fear of strangers, arises from the perception that the unknown plans and patterns of others may threaten our own well-being. Thus, as usual, pride and fear are two sides of the same coin. Accordingly, both chauvinism and xenophobia have contributed to negative views about other cultures.

By envisioning society as a divinely inspired coalition of church, custom, and state, Christendom intensified cultural chauvinism in the West by giving all sorts of particular cultural developments a divine and political stamp of approval. As a result, people were likely to be more forgiving of their own group and more critical of other groups. Formed by the prevailing assumptions of their own societies, missionaries from Europe and North America interpreted the relative lack of technological development and political power they saw among peoples in Asia, Africa, and Latin America as confirmation that they came from superior societies. They concluded that they were obligated to share western civilization's modes of clothing, education, medicine, agriculture, and industry.

William Carey's memorable phrase, "poor, barbarous, naked pagans as destitute of civilization as they are of true religion," expresses important dimensions of the negative stereotyping of other cultures. Civilization, not culture, was the key concept in mission thinking about other societies in the nineteenth century. Africans and the primal peoples of the

Americas were regarded as uncivilized, probably because they lacked writing and the wheel, hence were "destitute." In these areas, missionaries often saw themselves as going into a vacuum, where whatever they brought was a gift to the natives. Asian peoples were acknowledged to be civilized, but missionaries often saw themselves called to do battle with cultures they regarded as corrupt. In either situation, they felt called to remedy what was defective, "a degradation of humanity," in Knight-Bruce's words.

Few missionaries have exactly "equated Christianity with western civilization," as a common charge would have it, and some cautioned that "civilizing" activities could distract them from spiritual work. However, many in the nineteenth century saw the two as companions, with the gospel making a way for civilization. American A. J. Gordon, a Baptist, put it thus:

> Civilization without the gospel cannot effect any permanent uplift in non-Christian society, while the gospel without civilization can completely transform and humanize society.... Civilization and social amelioration are wrapped up in the gospel in germ, even as the oak is wrapped up in the acorn.... The word of God is the seed-corn of social morality, of material prosperity, and of human civilization.[1]

Rejoicing in a new receptivity to the West in Africa and Asia, the Domestic and Foreign Missionary Society of the Episcopal Church declared in 1899 that

> a crisis presents itself that makes it the imperative duty of the Church of God to go at once and possess these lands in the name of Christ. The doors are now open wide and many, yea hun-

dreds, are lifting up their hands and asking for our religion, our civilization, our schools.[2]

The massive brutality of World War I, a conflict incited and prosecuted by "Christian nations," prompted significant reassessment of the supposed superiority of the Global North. In the 1920s, Daniel Fleming, an American Presbyterian missiologist, called for eradicating the superiority complex he saw in mission work and set the stage for much of the thinking that would unfold in the twentieth century. Using the anthropologically neutral term "culture," not the ideologically freighted term "civilization," he declared that the idea of racial superiority was the root of the sense of cultural superiority, which, in turn, was the root of the idea of religious superiority. Calling for mutuality in giving and receiving between East and West, he outlined a "four-fold struggle in love", in which each group would attempt to see and appreciate admirable qualities in other people; to detect elements in other people that hinder progress; to detect elements in their own culture worthy of transplanting; and to detect elements in their own culture that would harm other people.[3] Today this sounds commonplace, but it was new thinking at the time.

∿ Mission and Colonialism

Colonialism's link with western mission sharpens concern about whether mission is itself a kind of cultural imperialism. State-imposed Christianity, whether by edict or military violence, is the most blatant expression of Christian religious imperialism, as we have seen in the Christendom of the Roman period, the conversion of Europe, the Crusades, and the Spanish conquest of the Americas. Modern European colonialism highlights more subtle dynamics.

The advance of nations of the Global North into societies of the Global South, together with the advent of Christian missionaries, shaped the dilemmas faced by the Two-Thirds World martyrs we met in chapter four. Manche Masemola's Christian faith might not have been fatally offensive to her parents if its arrival had not coincided roughly with British control over Sekhukhuneland, and she might have grown old as a Christian grandmother. Alternatively, without the colonial incursion, she might never have become a Christian, either because no missionary influence would have reached her or because the gospel might not have appeared so compelling without an apparently invincible world power behind it. Would Lucian Tapiedi have been killed if he had not been traveling with white missionaries, or if he had not been part of a church system brought to Papua New Guinea by the Global North?

Returning to the "mass movement toward Christianity" in Manicaland in the twentieth century's first decade, which we reviewed in chapter two, is it not significant that rebellions by the indigenous peoples of Rhodesia were twice put down, in 1893 and 1896, by the British South Africa Company created by Cecil Rhodes, the British imperial adventurer who promised to "paint Africa [British] red from Capetown to Cairo"? Since the two chief spirit mediums of the Shona people were executed after the second rebellion, did the churches not benefit from the indigenous religion's violent collapse, although they were not formally linked to the military campaign? And since the various churches, including the Anglicans, received large tracts of land from Cecil Rhodes for rural missions, might not the churches' resulting socio-political power have also influenced the "mass movement"?

Such questions can be posed by skeptics to argue that Christianity's spread has been fundamentally pernicious in human history. They can also be posed by Christians who are open to mission involvement but who are deeply concerned about mission legacies from the past and possible dangers in the future. At the opening of the twenty-first century, the United States sits astride the globe as no nation has in human history, projecting enormous political, economic, and cultural influence over the entire world. Is it possible for Americans to engage in world mission today without in some way being complicit in that projection of power, even if unwittingly? Beyond the issue of the United States, is it possible that religious mission from the Global North is simply a vehicle of northern power, privilege, and arrogance—in short, neo-colonialism? Might not cultural influence be the most pervasive form of that power?

The history of mission's relation to colonialism is one that calls for _both-and_ thinking, not _either-or_. We can neither wholly condemn nor wholly absolve Christian mission in its relationship with colonial powers. Mission happened differently in different places, at different times, with various kinds of people. Often missionaries arrived well before western governments became involved in the territories concerned, so the common impression that the gospel arrived in tandem with the power and protection of colonialism is exaggerated. Furthermore, a minority of western missionaries deplored and opposed colonialism in all its forms. Arthur Shearly Cripps was one such in Rhodesia, and there he was joined by two or three in other Christian denominations. Similarly, only a minority of missionaries believed that colonial powers were God's instruments for propagating western civilization and that missionaries were called to be partners in that enterprise. As Stephen Neill puts it:

> The majority probably have held a view somewhere between the two extremes. Missionaries, like all other human beings, are men and women of their time. A century ago the extension of western dominance was seen to be irresistible. Many accepted it as something undesirable in itself, but were willing to make the best of a situation they would not have freely chosen. Others, seeing some good in occupation by a western power, were prepared to accept it for the sake of the good, but sometimes to turn all too blind an eye to the evil.[4]

Some missionaries both cooperated with colonial power as a matter of daily routine and strenuously opposed particular policies such as slave trading, forced labor, liquor sales, and apartheid. Many recent missionaries have so appreciated the people among whom they work that they have become very critical of their own cultures. Ironically, the missionary sometimes becomes more attached to a people's older and "unspoiled" culture than the people themselves, who may be eager to appropriate the education and lifestyle of westerners.

Looking to the present and future, it may be reassuring to know that the lessons of colonialism are probably the lessons that today's missionaries have taken to heart most keenly, certainly among Anglicans. If today's Anglican missionaries have one common anxiety, it is of behaving in any way that could be remotely perceived as imperialist, neo-colonial, or culturally condescending. Of course, such a sensibility does not guarantee error-free mission, but a basic sensitivity has been instilled by general awareness and specific training experiences. Today, servant-hood and partnership have become central in Anglican missionary consciousness, and they have borne rich fruit in relationships with international companions.

The other source of reassurance is that our international companions are at least as sensitive to cultural colonialism as any critic in the Global North, and they do not hesitate to address the issue when they see it. Gone, fortunately, are the days when a missionary could behave badly with impunity, blissfully unaware of giving offense. Equally important, the liberation movements of the twentieth century demonstrate that it is simply not the case that peoples in other parts of the world were unaware of the harmful effects of some missionary attitudes. Nor, with few exceptions, is it the case now that peoples are vulnerable to being harmed unawares. To suppose otherwise is simply to replace the old-style condescension with a new-style one, both regarding "natives" as naively unable to interpret and evaluate their experience of the wider world. The colonial experience must forever chasten Christian mission, but with the twin checks of self-awareness and indigenous critique it can yet go forward, especially as we grow in understanding the dynamics of culture.

∿ Understanding Culture

What *is* culture? Here is a working definition. *Culture consists of the social patterns and material objects through which people interact to express and organize themselves.* Culture thus includes many different social practices, techniques, and symbols, as well as skills and artifacts such as writing and literature, music and art, tools and machines, and crafted objects. It involves the historically and socially transmitted ways in which people interact with their own practices and products to communicate, celebrate, and get work done.

This way of understanding culture focuses on the interaction between people and what they have created, not on the artifacts themselves. In other words, it is *in the interaction* that people experience meaning; the meaning of an object, a practice, or a symbol is not something contained in that item, just waiting to be unpacked. No, the experience of meaning arises from what the person doing the unpacking brings to the encounter as well as from the item itself. We know this from ordinary experience. The same piece of music induces in one person a mood of joyful expectation and in another a wistful melancholy. One person's city of opportunity is another's urban nightmare. A Sunday Bible study class can elicit widely differing interpretations of a single parable or story.

Diversity of interpretation within shared cultural experience can have major ethical, social, and political ramifications. Harriet Beecher Stowe's classic *Uncle Tom's Cabin* helped catalyze the anti-slavery campaign in nineteenth-century America, while for twentieth-century African Americans just the name "Uncle Tom" became a byword for servile complicity. Art shows become controversial when one community's art is another community's pornography and sacrilege. People who share a commitment to feminism can disagree radically about the implications of particular books, social patterns, or court decisions.

This diversity highlights several important features of human cultures. First, cultures change constantly through the varying interpretations made by individuals and groups within them. Many people assume that cultures in the Two-Thirds World were uniform and unchanging before the impact of the modern West, while in fact they were changing a good deal.

For example, the migration of Bantu peoples from east Africa into southern Africa sometime in the first millennium multiplied the number of black societies and languages and largely displaced the San peoples. The ethos of India was shaped profoundly by the sixteenth-century invasion of the Moguls, who brought Islam and constructed monuments like the Taj Mahal. Increased communication around the world today means that cultures are changing more rapidly now, but no culture has ever been static.

Second, culture is a dialogue among various perspectives and communities, and is not based on a single voice. Thus it is a mistake to generalize too broadly about a culture, for every culture has competing subcultures. For instance, men in some African societies are seeking to recover polygamy, which they consider to be a more authentic African family pattern than monogamy. Some African women agree that polygamy was common in their societies, but they declare that it demeans women and impoverishes children. That is an internal cultural dialogue. It is similarly important to avoid stereotyping, whether negatively or positively. "Africans are relaxed"—and yet some of the most hard-driving managers I have known have been in Africa. "Indians are contemplative"—but you will not see that on market day! "Japanese are indirect"—but plenty of business transactions in Japan are abrupt. "Americans are rude"—but just compare the stately deliberations of the United States Senate with the cat-calls of the British House of Commons! Generalizations help us simplify reality, but they often do not reflect the full story.

Third, the interactive view of culture means that culture includes the contemporary as well as the traditional, the new as well as the old. People often reserve the term "culture" for some previous state of a society that they idealize as its authentic and true identity. Contemporary values and practices are viewed not as that society's culture but as a corruption or confusion of a pristine indigenous state. We might call this the nostalgia motif in popular cultural thinking. As we wrestle with new technologies and lifestyles, people in Europe and North America often long for earlier cultural patterns and disparage the confusing present. Projecting this nostalgia abroad, they idealize earlier periods of other cultures and grieve the impact of modern developments there. Some within other cultures are likewise nostalgic about their own societies prior to contact with the West.

There is much to treasure in local traditions and much to oppose in the current globalizing of Euro-American norms. Yet sheer nostalgia tends to be neither accurate nor useful in thinking about cultures. Imagining an unchanging past is not accurate, nor is imagining a past free of suffering and oppression. In the American context, there is little integrity in nostalgia for social patterns that were built, for instance, on white supremacy and male domination. Astute members of other societies are likewise skeptical of uncritical idealizations of their own past. Her six daughters' Shona names, says Mildred Mbwando, not only express Christian identity but also challenge Shona patriarchy: "The names express acceptance because, whilst the culture would appreciate a boy over a girl, we wanted to show that the girls were welcome and loved, for they all come from the Lord."

Excluding contemporary developments from "authentic culture" in favor of a mythical "tradition" dismisses the ongoing creativity within a society. Take two examples. The Indian film industry has for many years been the most prolific in the world, turning out a phenomenal number of movies. Yes, cinema is a modern western invention, but Indian films are most decidedly Indian, and film is now an important and fascinating aspect of Indian culture. Similarly, Afropop, the popular rock music generated by musicians throughout Africa and the Caribbean, is certainly modern in that it incorporates electric guitars, amplification, and musical influences from the West. Yet musically it is so distinctly African that the term "Afropop" was coined, and it voices important contemporary realities in those regions. Our cultural reflections are useful only if we realize that the new is as much a part of culture as the old.

~ Culture in Theological Perspective

With these understandings about culture, how can we relate culture and faith? It is helpful to realize at the outset that Christianity is not identical with any culture, western or otherwise. The gospel originated not in western culture but in the Jewish culture of the ancient Middle East. Jesus was a Jew of the first century, and his behavior and teaching bear the marks of his cultural context. At the same time, Jesus challenged his culture when he saw prevailing norms violating what he understood to be God's will, as in the treatment of women, poor people, lepers, and Samaritans. As the gospel spread in the Mediterranean world it began to bear the marks of Hellenistic culture at the same time that it challenged that culture at specific points. The same phenomenon occurred in Europe, though there the development of Christendom crippled the self-critical reflex for centuries.

A paradox begins to emerge here. The gospel is not identical with any culture, but the gospel must be expressed in terms that are culturally conditioned if it is to be expressed at all. This is so because we human beings are creatures of our cultures. Everything we do bears the imprint of culture. So also, the gospel is inevitably expressed through a culture. If this is a weakness, it is precisely the weakness God undertook in the incarnation, for the word did not become flesh in a transcultural or non-cultural human being, which would be impossible, but in one named Jesus, a Jew of Palestine. This incarnational dynamic is, in fact, Christianity's saving word to all human cultures, for although every culture is judged by the gospel, every culture is also regarded as a worthy vehicle of the gospel. The gospel of Jesus Christ transcends culture, certainly, but no single expression of that gospel can claim to be free of culture. Even as we try to define what the gospel is apart from culture, we must expect that any definition will be shaped by the culture of the speaker. That cultural expression has the potential for distorting the gospel through cultural limitations but also for illuminating the gospel through cultural insights.

Out of the critique of western mission's cultural impact comes an urgency that the gospel be proclaimed in such a way that it takes root and becomes expressed through the culture of the receiving people, not through the proclaimer's culture. Writing from his mission experience in China in 1912, the English Anglican Roland Allen grieved that

> our missions are in different countries among people of the most diverse characteristics, but all bear a most astonishing resemblance one to another. If we read the history of a mission in China we have only to change a few names and the same history will serve as the history of a mission in Zululand. There has been no new revelation. There has been no new discovery of

new aspects of the Gospel, no new unfolding of new forms of Christian life.[5]

In fact, more was happening under the radar of missionaries, but Allen's expectations of what could and should happen were radical and prophetic. In proposing a "Christ of the Indian Road" in 1925, E. Stanley Jones shared that expectation:

> Every nation has its peculiar contribution to make to the interpretation of Christianity. The Son of man is too great to be expressed by any one portion of humanity. Those that differ from us most will probably contribute most to our expression of Christianity.[6]

To Max Warren, general secretary of the Church Missionary Society after the mid-twentieth century, is attributed the saying, "It takes the whole world to know the whole gospel." There is no finished understanding of Christ waiting to be delivered and received. We are invited, instead, to journey into the mystery of the Christ who will appear uniquely to every individual and culture. We are invited, as well, to invite others in other cultures to experience that mystery in eager expectation of how Christ may appear uniquely to them, and in joyful anticipation of how their experience will enlarge our own.

Mission thought over the past forty years has suggested a number of terms for reflecting on how the gospel takes root in cultures. "Accommodation" is sometimes used, but it implies that the gospel is only reluctantly making concessions to the receiving culture. "Adaptation" is more helpful, but it describes relatively superficial ways in which the gospel takes on local features. "Enculturation" has become the most common term, suggesting a mutual interaction between gospel and culture at the level of symbol and meaning, so that the cultural setting sheds new light on the gospel even as it is affected by the gospel. "Indigenization" often denotes the transfer of church responsibility and control to local leaders. In theology, indigenization reformulates Christian truth through the symbols and categories of a national or regional culture. "Contextualization" extends the scope of this process to the social struggles and power relations of society. "Incarnation" uses the model of God's word becoming flesh to suggest that the gospel embraces culture as it is expressed through local idioms.

Roman Catholic theologian Robert Shreiter stresses that all theology is *local theology*, which means that no particular sector of world Christianity has a right to claim that its theological understanding is universally valid.[7] In particular, it is clear that the period of western control over how Christian faith is formulated and lived is over. New voices and new forms of Christian life have emerged in the cultures of Africa, Asia, and Latin America. What Christians around the world do share in common is the Christian story as found in the scriptures and, for many Christians, the creeds. Understanding what this story means is the work of theology, which does not come ready-made but is constructed from local materials. Theology is now a global conversation in which diverse individuals and groups share insight from how they have experienced Christ in their social, cultural, and political situations.

～ The Gospel Taking Root in a Culture

Illustrating the dynamics of a new form of Christian life emerging from culture is the night vigil movement I have experienced and studied in Zimbabwe. Early in my time at Bonda, lay leaders asked me if they could convene a *pungwe*, during which people stay up all night singing and preaching. As the event unfolded I was amazed at the number of people involved, the passion of the preaching, the strength of the singing, and, of course, the endurance of several hundred men, women, and children worshiping from dusk to dawn. Soon the *pungwe* became frequent at Bonda for youth gatherings, Mothers' Union inductions, stewardship initiatives, men's revivals, and major church festivals. I realized that this was a widespread movement. When Manicaland Anglicans wanted to accomplish something major spiritually and communally they turned to the *pungwe* as the most natural and power-ful vehicle. It turned out the movement was renewing many church traditions following the devastation of the Liberation War that brought independence in 1980.

The movement's power arose from its roots in Shona religion, culture, and history. In *Chivanhu*, the ancient practice of the Shona people, night is the best time for meeting the familial and territorial spirits of the ancestors, who are the practical focus of religious devotion. Energized by the possession rituals of spirit mediums, family and clan groups stay up all night for ceremonies full of singing, dancing, libations of ritual beer, drumming, and oracular utterances by the medi-ums. With such expectations that spiritual encounter and communal solidarity happen especially at night, early Shona converts to Christianity wanted to cele-brate their Christianity in all-night vigils as well as on Sundays. Early missionaries, however, prohibited such gatherings in church buildings because they feared that night worship would draw people back to the spirits. So for decades people held Christian night vigils more privately in homes in the outlying villages.

The missionaries defined acceptable Anglican worship as prayer book liturgy, led by designated leaders at scheduled times during daylight hours, for congregations meeting in specially designated church buildings. The people loved prayer book liturgy, but the magnetism of the night drew them to gatherings that included extemporaneous worship as well as prayer book liturgies. Anglican practice was being changed by indigenous culture, although on the edges of official church life. The night vigil of *Chivanhu* was being drawn into Christian practice for its culturally formed power to catalyze spiritual encounter and communal solidarity, but now the content was trinitarian Christianity.

Then came the Liberation War of the 1970s. Marxist-trained guerrillas held all-night rallies during which they instructed rural peasants in the dynamics of colonialism, proclaimed the goals of liberation, and generated enthusiasm for the war effort. In building on both the *pungwe* of *Chivanhu* and on vigils held in the churches before the war, the guerrillas demonstrated the adaptability of the *pungwe* and linked the practice with liberation. Perceiving the churches as allies of the Rhodesian regime, guerrillas often denounced Jesus at the rallies and shut down church operations. Retribution against suspected government collaborators sometimes included public executions and left many people with traumatic memories of the war-time rallies.

Yet the spiritual power, communal intensity, and liberation ethos of the wartime *pungwe* so energized people that Anglicans and other Christians after the war turned the *pungwe* into a primary vehicle of community life, theological development, church growth, mission outreach, and social liberation throughout Zimbabwe. Appropriation and transformation are the keynotes of what is happening. Indigenous religious culture is being appropriated by Christian tradition and transformed into a Christian vehicle. Conversely, Christianity is being transformed as its worship is influenced by preexisting rites and the indigenous culture highlights specific theological features such as the Holy Spirit and confrontation with evil powers.

This story takes us well beyond the missionary era and the narrow issue of what stance the missionary takes toward culture. In the emergence of authentic Christian life in communities around the world, the missionary is significant but scarcely the most important factor. People in the receiving cultures are the principal actors. Their cultures, like all cultures, are interactive processes that are resilient in the midst of change. Night vigils in the churches grew out of ancient religious practice, but they became part of faithful and theologically orthodox church life. Missionary opposition retarded their development temporarily but could not stop them. A modern guerrilla war worked unexpected changes on the practice and spurred its explosive growth into a central phenomenon of Shona Christian culture. Not all gospel-culture interactions are so dramatic, but the rooting of gospel in cultures around the world is happening in abundance. Consistently we find that cultures are powerfully dynamic, and that the gospel is also.

∾ The Other in Religion and Culture

Mission consists in crossing borders to meet the other, so we have focused on the encounter with other religions and other cultures. One of the deepest and most enduring patterns of Christian mission is that meeting the other brings us to more authentic encounter with ourselves, in our strength and our weakness, in our sight and our blindness. Mission also brings us to more authentic encounter with the God whom we share with the other, the God who shares us with each other.

As we meet other religions with incarnational expectancy, we are alert for the movements of God. The encounter highlights our own poverty and unfaithfulness and renews the call to prayer. At the same time, God's call to witness means, in the words of Paul, that "we do not proclaim ourselves; we proclaim Jesus Christ as Lord and ourselves as your slaves for Jesus' sake" (2 Corinthians 4:5). Witnessing to the One beyond us invites our freedom and our joy.

As we meet other cultures, we understand that the gospel challenges our own culture, and we strive to live and offer an authentic gospel undistorted by that background. Missioners also realize, however, that Christ may be expressed authentically through their own cultural personality as well. Just as we discover the gospel in a different way through Christians from other cultures who come to us, so our own individual and cultural perspective on the gospel can be a source of discovery for those who live in other countries and cultures. This invites freedom in the Spirit to be who one truly is, for, as St. Irenaeus declared, "The glory of God is a person fully alive." As we oscillate between critical self-examination and joyful freedom, we can trust that our hearers and co-workers will be able through the Spirit to discern the difference between real gospel and cultural baggage. And, in fact, they usually do!

"Our first task in approaching another people, another culture, another religion," wrote Max Warren, "is to take off our shoes, for the place we are approaching is holy. Else we may find ourselves treading on men's dreams. More serious still, we may forget that God was here before our arrival."[8]

Chapter Seven

A Vision for Mission in the Twenty-First Century

In the Anglican Diocese of Mpwapwa in Tanzania, Bishop Simon Chiwanga preaches during a eucharist that concludes a three-day retreat for his diocesan staff. Two Episcopal missionaries who have recently arrived from the United States to teach at the diocesan seminary are in the assembly. In his sermon the bishop, at the time also chair of the worldwide Anglican Consultative Council, rejoices in how the diocese is being encouraged by missionaries from abroad, who bring a "contagious" faith and give him great hope for the church.[1]

In a different African setting, an American missionary hiding with persecuted Christians in the Nuba Mountains of Sudan wonders aloud whether he should leave, lest his presence provoke attacks by the Muslim forces of the north. His Sudanese companions laugh and tell him, "The morale of the Christians has never been higher in the Nuba Mountains, because five Christians came to bring us physical supplies and the word of God. We are so happy that we have not been forgotten nor forsaken. You have been a witness to our suffering. We simply ask you to tell the world."[2]

A missionary priest with the Episcopal Anglican Church of Brazil, Patricia Powers, writes home to her friends and supporters in the United States:

> What is taking most of my time now is the preparation of seven mission encounters that are being held in each of the seven dioceses from June till December. Each encounter is programmed to deal with a different area of mission according to the need of each diocese. . . . I will be visiting Rondonia, a new area where we are implanting the Church. It has been many years since the Brazilian Church has considered entering into the missionary field again. I am told that I might have to get on a horse because we are so far in the interior of the country.[3]

Contagious faith. Witness to suffering. Outreach to new areas. These are several of the many faces of Christian mission today within and beyond the Anglican Communion. These are faces of God's mission in the world. Incarnationally, we can say even that these are faces of Christ on mission in the world.

✎ Ten Marks of Mission

In this book we have considered biblical bases for mission and surveyed the history of mission. With an emerging theology of mission, we have wrestled with the issues of other religions and cultures. Now it is time to develop a vision for mission that is both faithful to the past and open to the future of what God may be up to in the world.

This chapter highlights ten marks, or qualities, that I believe Anglican global mission should and will have in the coming decades. As churches and as individuals, Anglicans on mission in the twenty-first century will:

1. Proclaim the gospel with baptismal confidence.
2. Serve as sacraments of Christ in relationship.
3. Live as companions in solidarity with the suffering.
4. Receive Christ as pilgrims with others.
5. Nurture human wholeness in grassroots communities.
6. Struggle for jubilee justice, reconciliation, and peace.
7. Collaborate with other churches and Christian groups.
8. Explore gospel expression in diverse cultures.
9. Cooperate with people of other faiths.
10. Celebrate eucharistic community.

1. Proclaim the gospel with baptismal confidence.
Acting out gospel stories on a sidewalk is not every Episcopalian's idea of witness, but it was a transforming experience for a suburban teenager from Massachusetts on a summer mission in Mexico. Reporting on her trip, she was moved to tears as she described how a woman in Chihuahua committed her life to Christ after watching the youths mime one of Jesus' parables. We do not know the woman's religious background, but she was so touched by sheer and simple witness to the story of Jesus that she started a new chapter in her life.

The word "evangelism" is based on the word *evangel*, which, in turn, comes from the Greek word *euangellion*, which means "good news," or "gospel." So evangelism is "gospel-ism" or "good-news-ism"! Since the New Testament stresses proclaiming the gospel, evangelism is associated with telling the good news of what God has done in Christ through the Holy Spirit.

A well-known definition of evangelism by William
Temple, Archbishop of Canterbury in the 1940s, was
adapted by the Episcopal Church's General
Convention in 1973:

> The presentation of Jesus Christ, in the power of
> the Holy Spirit, in such ways that persons may
> be led to believe in Him as Saviour, and follow
> Him as Lord within the fellowship of His
> Church.[4]

"Telling our story in the light of God's story" is a sim-
pler understanding of evangelism suggested by
Donald Bitsberger, formerly an Episcopal missionary.
It is a story that creates Christian identity and story-
telling that anchors Christian witness. The sacrament
of baptism is where our own story mystically joins
the story of Christ in his death and resurrection and
where we are initiated into the vast community of
story that is the church. There we are charged,
"Confess the faith of Christ crucified, proclaim his resurrection, and share with us in his eternal priesthood"
(BCP 308). In other words, tell the story, whether to
the person next door or to an unevangelized villager
in Kazakhstan!

The Anglican Communion's Decade of Evangelism
(1990-2000) was a mixture of success and failure,
with the unfortunate result that many continue to
distrust calls to evangelize. Evangelism is simply the
personal gift of offering in love and joy one's own
experience of God. God's story gets told, not through
haranguing or prooftexting, but through humbly
opening one's own life in vulnerability to another. If
our witness is truly an encounter, we are also vulnerable to hearing the other person's story, which always
enlarges our own. This personal encounter bridges the
gap we may sense between the universality of the

truth we know in Christ and the experience of God others may have in different religious journeys. Christ may challenge some religious options and complete or confirm others. Evangelism aims not to debate doctrines but to bear witness to God come near through the intimate suffering and empowering love of Christ.

Vulnerability in telling and listening must be joined to vulnerability in doing, which means reaching out to touch and struggle with real needs, real hungers, real oppressions. Thus pastoral care and justice work walk hand in hand with evangelism, whether in a Peruvian *barrio*, a South African *kraal*, or a city ghetto anywhere. With such concern for the whole person, evangelism is not necessarily the main focus of every outreach, but it is essential in the overall mission of the church.

2. Serve as sacraments of Christ in relationship.

The notion that missionaries—and Christians in general, for that matter!—serve as sacraments may startle you, but it discloses much of what mission is. Sacraments, the Catechism tells us, are "outward and visible signs of inward and spiritual grace" (BCP 857). We are used to thinking of baptism as the sacrament of new birth and eucharist as the sacrament of the body and blood of Christ. These and other sacramental rites, such as marriage, ordination, confirmation, reconciliation, and anointing of the sick, derive their meaning from the larger reality that the church itself is a sacrament, an outward and visible sign of Christ's continuing presence in the world through a community.

A Christian on mission, then, is a sacrament of God's mission to reconcile all people with one another and with God in Christ. It is the humble spirit of serving that reveals this movement of God through a missioner's personality and work. Rejecting the colonial past, Anglican missioners today have turned away from authoritarian patterns and now seek to live into Jesus' words, "I came not to be served but to serve." Listening to local needs and working under indigenous leaders will only intensify in the coming decades.

A sacramental emphasis on persons helps both missionaries and sending groups to retain an incarnational focus on relationships among people in community, where God truly lives and where the most lasting impacts are made. For Christians in the Global North, money and electronics are tempting alternatives today. As the gap widens between the prosperous north and the poor south, sending money can seem more efficient and therefore more responsible than sending and receiving people, who have sensitive feelings, hidden weaknesses, and potential illnesses. Money can get work done and it is a crucial expression of stewardship, but it causes at least as many misunderstandings as people on the ground do. Since about 1970 mainline denominations in the Global North have focused more on making grants than on sending personnel, but interchurch relations have continued to be complex, and churches in the Global South have sometimes felt cut off from relationship.

God's nature is to form relationships and build community, and the church's mission must reflect that priority. It is marvelous how communication and relationship are fostered around the world electronically, and the world-wide web provides huge troves of information. Ultimately, however, there is no substitute for being together. E-mail, video, DVD, online talk, and whatever will follow them help a great deal, but they will no more replace the incarnation of real people being with real people than the telephone, radio, or tape recorder did. Conversely, when the missionary's own inner voices insinuate that the mission would be valid if only there were more money, more equipment, more buildings, more programs, I want to say, "You yourself are a precious sacrament. The people to whom you have come are sacraments. Your relationships are holy. That is enough."

The missionary in any place is a sacrament of the gospel's universality—the fact that it transcends cultural, geographic, and linguistic boundaries to create communities in Christ. Colonialism abroad and xenophobia at home gave the term "foreigner" a negative connotation, but the reality is that every Christian community needs a few foreigners. Anyone whose experience is broader than the particular setting, for whom that place is not really home, provides the community with a third point of reference between itself and the gospel, much as surveyors and navigators need triangulation points to determine their position. Sensing this, congregations in Britain and North America in recent years have taken to calling the international Christians in their midst missionaries, not because these Christians have come with an explicit mission intention but because their very presence fulfills a mission function. Foreigners help keep us close to what the gospel is and close to the presence of Christ.

3. Live as companions in solidarity with the suffering.

Reflecting on church relationships around the world, the Anglican Communion's Mission Commission concluded in 1999:

> We suggest that the time has come to shift the focus in those relationships from *partnership*, which in many cases has taken on the flavour of a business relationship characterised by pro-

grammes and financial priorities, to *companion-ship*, which speaks of the priority of relation-ships, of sharing in solidarity.[5]

Shift from partnership to companionship? The difference between the two may seem so subtle as to be scarcely worth the trouble. Yet the shift is important. Despite the ideals of MRI (Mutual Responsibility and Interdependence in the Body of Christ) and PIM (Partnership in Mission), disparities in money and power between the Global North and the Global South continue to skew relations as the north directs policy and condescends toward the south. Partnership is a biblical concept, but its legal and business connotations in contemporary English can distort the mission lifestyle we seek.

The Latin root of the word "companion" is "with bread." A companion is someone with whom we share bread, someone close enough to us and with us long enough on a journey so that we eat together. We may be pursuing a task or an errand, but companionship highlights our being together rather than the work or the goal. Companionship in mission, then, moves goals and resources between Anglican provinces to the background, and highlights simply being together—discovering one another and exploring new friendships. Since the early 1970s the companion diocese movement has become the principal way that ordinary Anglicans have discovered one another around the communion, and the companionship principle applies equally to parish-to-parish and interprovincial links. Embracing a similar concept, the Evangelical Lutheran Church in America uses "accompaniment" as its paradigm for mission in the twenty-first century and encourages companion synod relationships.[6]

Solidarity is the shape companionship takes when the other is suffering. Suffering is something we all want to avoid, so there is a natural human tendency to stand back from someone who is suffering, lest the trouble overtake us as well. Solidarity involves a deliberate decision to stand *with* the companion in trauma and share the burden, whatever it may be. Solidarity is different from trying to solve the problems causing the trauma. Sometimes something can be done, sometimes nothing. Regardless, solidarity means identifying oneself with our companion's suffering, being there physically if possible, but also offering love, prayer, and communication from a distance.

Living in a rural community in the turmoil of El Salvador in the early 1990s was a challenge for Daniel Moss and Tyler Haaren, a mission couple sponsored by the Diocese of Massachusetts. They sought to help with community-organizing, but their main intention was simply to be there with the Salvadorans. They shared the people's physical deprivations, fear of further violence, and frustration with corrupt bureaucrats. They listened to the *Contra* war stories that folks needed to tell as they sought healing from their trauma. The mission was solidarity. Similarly, in the late 1980s, the diocese offered sabbatical respite to South African clergy engaged in the anti-apartheid struggle. Simply offering sanctuary expressed solidarity.

Companionship and solidarity fulfill the essentially relational nature of God's mission. As we saw in the creation story, mission is not mainly a matter of fixing what is broken. Instead, building relationships in community is central. God came to be our companion in the incarnate Christ. It was Jesus' gentle companionship with two disciples on the road to Emmaus that inspired our evening prayer, "Lord Jesus, stay with us, for evening is at hand and the day is past; be our companion in the way..." (BCP 124). Solidarity is companionship in the way of the cross. As Jesus shared our suffering, we undertake to empty ourselves and share the suffering of others, all of us living as sacraments of Christ's presence.

4. Receive Christ as pilgrims with others.

"I feel that I've received so much more than I ever gave!" This is a remarkably consistent refrain today among missionaries, whether they are Anglican, Lutheran, Presbyterian, or Roman Catholic. Listen, for instance, to Episcopal missionary Stewart Lane:

> My thirty-five years in Malawi have brought me much joy and love, lots of adventure and not a little fear, taught me more and enriched me in more ways than I can express. It's been a good life and I am so thankful that we took the totally mad step of coming here. To add to that the hope, however faint, that I may actually have given something in return is sweet.[7]

I myself came back from Africa a different kind of Christian than when I went. Listening to unschooled Shona Christians testify to Christ before vast congregations taught me how to preach. Praying behind the mountain at dawn with a Marange Christian taught me about spiritual friendship. African congregations taught me how cohesive parish communities can be when supported by prayer and committed families.

The stress on receiving as well as giving in the partnership and companionship models of mission is no longer just an ideal but a major witness of missionaries today. The transforming spiritual experiences they celebrate suggest that pilgrimage is fundamental to what mission is and should be. A pilgrim is someone who undertakes an intentional journey to deepen his or her experience of God. All of life, of course, is a pilgrimage in that we mature in Christ as we walk life's hills and valleys. Mission pilgrims seek a new experience of Christ through a people and culture different from their own. People, not places, are the focus of the mission pilgrimage. We become pilgrims in Christ through the revelations of another people's life in Christ.

Receiving Christ as pilgrims with others applies not only to outgoing missionaries but to the church as a whole, as we receive mission outreach from other parts of the world. This type of receiving is more an ideal than a reality as the new century opens. Financial pressures limit the ability of Asian, African, and Latin American Christians to send missionaries to a Global North that needs their fresh spirituality. Northern mission agencies have responded by funding both south-to-north and south-to-south missionary appointments, such as a priest from the Dominican Republic doing pastoral work in Spain and a South Indian presbyter teaching in an African seminary. Increasingly, conference and retreat leaders are brought from the Global South. For instance, Benjamin Kwashi, bishop of the Diocese of Jos in Nigeria, keynoted New Wineskins for Global Mission 2000, the Episcopal Church's largest mission conference. His topic? "From Maintenance to Mission"! As northern Christians experience the gifts of southern Christians in their midst, the coming decades will see a more robust commitment to receiving mission from our fellow pilgrims in Christ.

5. Nurture human wholeness in grassroots communities.

I never saw the Ethiopian button factory, but I imagine it vividly as described by Eleanor Vandevort, an

Episcopalian who served the Nuer people in Sudan through the Presbyterian Church. After conducting a study and consulting with the Ethiopian government, a United States government aid program determined in the 1950s that a button factory would spur economic development among the desperately poor local Ethiopians. A modern factory was built, and for a while it made buttons. Years later Eleanor passed by the site. Weeds had taken over, millions of buttons were scattered over the ground, and looking out through a broken factory window was a goat!

The button factory was typical of many "Third World development" strategies devised after 1950. The technological prowess and financial might of the Global North encouraged social planners and development experts to dream big dreams and generate large-scale projects to address poverty and disease around the world. Human progress was expected through modernization, getting the "undeveloped" Global South to travel the same road the Global North had traveled toward industrialization and urbanization. Such macrocosmic thinking affected the churches, as newly independent and needy governments encouraged them to expand their already large investments in education and health. Strategies for church life were also large-scale, whether in evangelism, institution-building, or theological education by extension. Results were often less than spectacular, as with the button factory.

The costs that modernization has exacted in the community life and physical environment of the Global North should make us think twice about promoting it as a panacea for the Global South. We should be just as cautious with the concept of "development" itself. Like the now discredited concept of "civilization" as viewed in the nineteenth century, development tends to smuggle in an expectation that societies in the Global South should replicate the patterns of the Global North. Moreover, development projects have sometimes served as vehicles for the north's continuing exploitation of the south, with the result that the real quality of life of "developing" societies has deteriorated rather than improved. Globalization of the world economy has often had similar effects.

How different is the story of the Mothers' Union Development Center at Bonda in Zimbabwe! In the mothers' weekly prayers and testimonies, my wife Jane began to see that the women needed financial resources beyond their produce sales and the money their husbands sporadically sent home from city jobs, and she became *mupi wepfungwa*, a "giver of ideas." The cooperative was founded by the women themselves; it built on their common Anglican identity and was guided by prayer and worship together. Today the still growing center's indigenous fabric designs and clothing projects continue to generate income for many women. When Danish fact-finders asked the Bonda women why their center flourished while aid-sponsored centers faltered, the mothers replied, "Because we pray together!"

The women's center illustrates today's focus on the initiative of grassroots communities. Physical and economic wholeness fulfills the comprehensive scope of Jesus' ministry, so it is not simply a secular add-on to mission. Such wholeness, however, emerges best from *within* communities rather than from models imported from outside, for every situation is unique, and it is perilous to generalize from one context to another. While training and seed money are important, success depends on people generating vision themselves so that they own the project and take pride in it. Effective mission initiatives in health, education, and economics in the new century will work through local church communities with their incomparable resources of prayer, social cohesion, and shared vision. This grassroots approach is already focusing Anglican efforts to respond to the catastrophe of the AIDS pandemic, where it is clear that the church has a crucial motivational and spiritual contribution to make alongside epidemiological initiatives.[8]

Certain basic conditions are essential for human wholeness, like clean water, adequate food, medical care, educational opportunity, and economic viability. Christian mission in the twenty-first century is seeking ways to pursue these without imposing a new cultural and economic imperialism. Micro-enterprises, community loan funds, and localized health projects are helpful new initiatives, and others will emerge as time goes on.

6. *Struggle for jubilee justice, reconciliation, and peace.*

We renounce three kinds of evil when we are baptized: "Satan and all the spiritual forces of wickedness," our own sinful desires, and, between those two poles, "the evil powers of this world which corrupt and destroy the creatures of God" (BCP 302). That middle level highlights *systems* of evil, organized patterns of human behavior that inflict injustice and oppress others. Contemporary oppressions include racism and sexism, classism and heterosexism, slavery and economic exploitation, pornography and environmental pollution. In response, we covenant in our baptism to "strive for justice and peace among all people, and respect the dignity of every human being" (BCP 305).

At the opening of a new century and millennium, Jubilee 2000 coalesced an Anglican and ecumenical drive for justice and peace through the biblical jubilee imperatives of debt cancellation, environmental renewal, and human liberation (Leviticus 25 and Luke 4). In the midst of many mission efforts to empower the poor, the debt initiative seeks to address the staggering national debts that imprison millions of people in poverty. It also addresses systemic oppression in poor countries by making debt relief conditional on human rights, civilian rule, and the needs of the poor rather than the appetites of wealthy and military elites.

Jubilee helps focus our conviction that global mission must address not only specific kinds of suffering but also the underlying dynamics that produce such suffering. At the Transformation Center in Lesotho, for instance, longtime Episcopal missioners John and Judy Gay worked against apartheid through training people to analyze power dynamics and organize local communities. In Bangalore, India, ecumenical Christians serve the urban poor through a center called Divya Shanthi. The first mission volunteer sponsored by the Diocese of Massachusetts in the early 1990s was a human rights lawyer who risked her life in El Salvador to defend people being harassed by the government of the time.

"In Christ," the apostle Paul wrote, "God was reconciling the world to himself...and entrusting the message of reconciliation to us" (2 Corinthians 5:19). Reconciliation is emerging as a major focus of global mission in the new century. One of the most luminous legacies of the twentieth century is the work of the Truth and Reconciliation Commission in South Africa under the leadership of Anglican Archbishop Desmond Tutu. "No future without forgiveness" is Tutu's summary phrase for the commission's extraordinary effort to promote reconciliation in the aftermath of apartheid.[9] With the commission as an example, a Massachusetts missioner was asked to help reconcile Christians and Muslims trying to preserve a peace pact in the Philippines. In the wake of the genocide between Hutus and Tutsis in Rwanda, Sonja Hoekstra-Foss, a missioner with Episcopal World Mission, found her work deepened by the fact that her own family had perished in the Nazi holocaust. "The healing that is so needed here in Rwanda is reconciliation," she wrote.[10]

Justice enhances personal wholeness, and history demonstrates that in society there is no lasting peace without justice. Reconciliation may be the most crucial struggle, for between reconciled parties justice becomes a free gift rather than a negotiated concession, and reconciliation is itself a surrender to peace.

7. *Collaborate with other churches and Christian groups.*

In Beijing, Episcopal priest Elyn Macinnis pastors an ecumenical congregation of expatriates where her Anglican identity helps to unify in one fellowship Christians ranging from Southern Baptists to Presbyterians. In Muslim countries that prohibit any Christian assembly, mission companions sometimes pastor ecumenical congregations under such titles as "morale officer" or "community coordinator."

During Swahili language training in Tanzania, Episcopal missioners Joan and Lou Mattia celebrated their ecumenical context:

> The biggest churches working here are the Roman Catholics, Baptists, Anglicans, Lutherans, Moravians and a score of independent Pentecostal or smaller churches. It is truly amazing to see the kingdom at work through so

many hands. Our language class has Germans, Koreans, Americans, Indians, Polish and a South American. . . . The Body of Christ is truly larger than any one denomination and they all cooperate fairly well helping each other in the field. On Ash Wednesday we borrowed some palms from the Roman Catholics and made ashes in the school kitchen for the evening Lutheran service.[11]

Since most missionary training is conducted ecumenically, missionaries often have a more ecumenical perspective than, say, clergy trained in denominational seminaries.

"Do nothing alone that can be done together with others" is the gist of what the ecumenical movement has known as the Lund Principle since 1952. Fifty years later many churches accept each other's validity more fully than they once did. We recognize that in worship we can prefer something without insisting that it is "the right way," and we celebrate diverse liturgical styles. We may be strongly committed to a particular doctrine, but we can enter into Christian fellowship with those who believe differently. The main challenge today is not acceptance but actually doing things together. The desire of each church to express the fullness of the gospel prompts us to invest major resources of time, people, and money in the best programs we can devise in every conceivable type of mission. It can be hard to see that no one church can do all things equally well and that we enhance our witness to Christ when we pool resources with groups who have gifts in areas where we are weak.

Called to Common Mission is the document that ushered in full communion between the Episcopal Church and the Evangelical Lutheran Church in

America in 2000, as *The Porvoo Common Statement* of 1996 brought full communion between the Nordic and Baltic Lutheran churches and the British and Irish Anglican churches. Living into that call to common mission is a mandate not only for Anglican-Lutheran relations but for Anglican cooperation with all churches. Practical ecumenism at home will certainly stimulate ecumenism in global mission in the twenty-first century. Conversely, the Holy Spirit's movement in other places often brings Christians together in ways that teach us here at home. For example, the liveliest and most influential night vigils among Zimbabwean Christians are the ones that bring churches together, and rubbing shoulders with diverse Christians in Africa has made me more ecumenical in my work in the United States. Resource scarcity sometimes prompts collaboration that affects the home front. While traveling to Haiti I encountered a large group of doctors and nurses from a Presbyterian congregation in Virginia embarking on a short-term mission to L'Hopital St. Croix in Leogane, a major Episcopal institution. Such collaboration can only strengthen our common witness in Christ.

8. *Explore gospel expression in diverse cultures.*
Culture is a major dimension that Anglican global mission will explore in the twenty-first century, affecting how all of us experience Christ through the multicultural diversity of our world. Rejecting the ethnocentrism of the past, missioners today strive to grow into the culture of the people to whom they are called. For example, early in their mission service in Kenya, Tom and Barbara Lutton discovered how different Christmas was going to be:

> We are learning to be sensitive when asking
> questions here about gifts and celebrations. Gift
> giving is done but not at all on the scale of the
> American Christmas. Sweets and a new dress or
> pants and shirt are considered plenty; in fact,
> most children are lucky to receive that much.
> We have not heard any mention of gifts to hus-
> bands or wives and must assume most of the
> giving is to children and friends. Christmas is a
> time when everyone goes home to family. . . .
> Being with family is most important.[12]

The missionary goes as a learner of culture, not a
teacher. Sensitivity means having a vulnerable spirit
that perceives nuances of feeling and thought in others and is willing to mull them over and be affected by
them. Inquiring is an important way of learning, but
here the missionaries are saying they want to be careful even about how they phrase their questions, lest
they communicate disturbing assumptions.

Joy comes from discovering how Christ's gospel is
being revealed anew through the different ways people live. Recent Anglican growth among the Wichi
people of northern Argentina resulted in over a thousand confirmations annually and a new wave of ordi-
nations. I asked the bishop of that diocese, South
American Missionary Society appointee Maurice
Sinclair, what particular shape Wichi Christian spirituality has taken. In their experience of God, he said, the
Wichi treasure especially the Holy Spirit's protection
from evil spirits, such as those that a sorcerer invoked
(in vain!) on the first two Wichi converts. Also, the
Wichi language's difficulty with abstractions produced
novel renderings in the first Wichi Bible. "Eternal life,"
for instance, became "the fresh greenness that never
fades." What a revelation! It connects the biblical hope

of unending fellowship to the equally biblical confidence that the entire universe will be renewed, with implications for environmental theology.

The gospel challenges as well as affirms culture, as we saw in chapter six, and not every cultural expression is faithful to the gospel. For example, most Anglicans today oppose health-and-wealth versions of the gospel and any preaching that invokes God's favor on chauvinistic nationalism. Homosexuality is a contemporary issue on which Anglicans and many Christians disagree, both cross-culturally and within cultures, differing even about whether the issue is spiritual, moral, cultural, or all three. In such impasses, the Anglican way is a commitment to continue in conversation with one another, confident that through our common life God will guide us into the fullness of truth. Insisting on the primacy of mission, the Episcopal Church's Standing Commission on World Mission declared that doing mission together in the midst of such disagreements is not only possible but imperative for the church's witness.[13] The truly important intersections of gospel and culture in Christian history have always been anguished, but they have also been revelatory.

9. Cooperate with people of other faiths.
Mission in the new century must encourage church members in exploring the faith journeys of people who embrace other religions. A landscape of multiple religious options was home territory for Christians in the first century, as it is for Christians in the more recently evangelized areas of the Global South. It is only because options like Islam, Hinduism, and Buddhism are newly prominent in the Global North that a religiously plural environment *feels* to us like a new situation for Christianity. Similarly, northern

Christians are often less aware of the nature of other religions than Christians in the Global South—or their forebears in the first century. Global mission can only be strengthened by educational initiatives that enable people in the pews to understand more about world religions, preferably through direct contact with people of other faiths.

Everyone involved in global mission should also be exploring ways in which people of all faiths can cooperate in practical projects even as they disagree in their theologies. Flood and famine relief are obvious examples, as is the AIDS pandemic. Working together may engender deeper mutual understanding than seminars and conferences do. Joint action also expresses a humble recognition that, while the community of Jesus Christ plays an essential role in making Christ known explicitly, God's mission is not limited to the church. God may work not only through other religious people but, as church consultant Loren Mead suggests, through movements that are not primarily religious.[14]

The journey of interreligious understanding and joint action is entirely compatible with being faithful to the call to witness to Christ. The 1998 Lambeth Conference's Thirty Theses on Christian Responses to People of Other Faiths is a helpful blueprint of attitudes, relationships, theology, responses, and methods for growing in understanding. In the middle of it the bishops forthrightly endorse the fact that "Christians want to make Christ known and give others the opportunity of following him."[15]

As we grow in understanding people of other faiths, we become able to discern better the way forward in controversial interactions between religions. For instance, the question of whether ancestor veneration is a legitimate expression of the communion of the saints is hotly discussed by Christians in parts of Asia and Africa. We have seen how early missionaries among the Shona mistakenly equated any nocturnal worship with ancestral rites, but the role of the ancestors continues to be a live issue. What light can be shed on this by Christians and missioners in Korea who seek to understand shamanism, or those in Latin America who puzzle over the great popular festivals of the saints? Comparing and correlating other religions with Christian theology has preoccupied generations of missionaries and will continue to do so. The conundrums are difficult, but we can be confident that engaging them is part of the mission that God is carrying out with us.

10. Celebrate eucharistic community.

As mission begins with the baptismal charge to proclaim, it culminates in the eucharistic community that embodies all that we are called to become as God's people carrying out God's mission. Eucharist proclaims the history of God's saving work in the life, death, and resurrection of Jesus, who was God standing with us. It sacramentally brings that history forward into the present through the Lord's Supper, which echoes the incarnation by taking the real stuff of earth and making it a vessel of Christ's healing for human wholeness. Transformed into a community that includes all sorts and conditions of people, we are sent into the world to participate in God's mission of reconciliation in the power of the Holy Spirit. Despite all obstacles and setbacks we do not lose heart, because this eucharistic life points beyond itself to the consummation of all things in the future glory of the messianic banquet in heaven.

Eucharistic communities must be foundational in Anglican mission initiative and strategy in the twen-

ty-first century. God works in diverse ways beyond
the church, but the professing community of Christ
offers Christ's presence in the world explicitly and is
therefore essential. Gathering new Christians into
congregations, what is often called church-planting, is
a precious fruit of proclamation, as is the nurture of
existing communities. In the new century this is especially important in cities, where people often cannot
find community even though that is where over half
the world's people live. It is also crucial for the generations of young people now under twenty-five, who
constitute over half the population of the Global
South.

Perhaps the most moving eucharist I have been
part of was one celebrated with a Shona family beside
the smoldering ruins of their thatched home that had
been torched by government troops in a campaign to
evict squatters. After fighting in the Liberation War,
Gilbert Matinenga had settled on land he thought
belonged to his ancestors. Bringing their infant son to
Bonda to be baptized, Gilbert and his wife Farai had
named the child Freedom to celebrate the independence era. It turned out they were occupying land that
had been sold to an African middle-class family, and
on this day government troops came to burn them
out. Visiting them in the catastrophe, I loaded bags of
their harvested maize into the car to store at the
church. Then, on the cleared ground of the home-
stead, together with their now homeless neighbors
and with Freedom squalling in his mother's arms, we
celebrated the supper of the Lord and proclaimed
Christ's death and resurrection until he comes again.
I never saw that family again, but what we did there
that day seemed the mission of God in that place.

Visiting victims of Hurricane Mitch in Honduras,
Phoebe Griswold, spouse of the Episcopal Church's

presiding bishop, saw her outreach in eucharistic terms:

> Mud was everywhere. Homes were awash in it. People walked knee deep in slime. Another mud line was not only on the homes but on the people as well.... We, Episcopal Relief and Development and the Diocese of Honduras, under the leadership of Bishop Frade, traveled down washed out gullies and went where no other secular organization had been. We listened to people's stories. To be heard in such a crisis is in itself an act of healing. Also, we distributed food to families where the Diocese had a list of every name because they knew each family. I gave out bags of food, saying quietly to myself, "The Body of Christ."[16]

Eucharistic mission focuses on the self-giving presence of Christ and forms relationships of solidarity that, in turn, create luminous community in the world.

These ten marks of mission for the twenty-first century are ten *qualities* our mission should have, not ten *kinds* of mission. They are ten criteria or tests of our vision and our faithfulness. Every mission initiative has its own emphasis and cannot display all ten qualities equally. "Now there are varieties of gifts, but the same Spirit," wrote Paul the missionary (1 Corinthians 12:5). Yet the overall mission of the church should show forth these marks, and any particular initiative should enhance not only its own emphasis but the church's total witness.

Chapter Eight

Energizing Communities for Mission

I love being on All Angels' Mission Committee," wrote Louisa Turner in the newsletter of her parish, All Angels' Episcopal Church in New York City. "Being involved with missions is one of the most exciting, awesome and important things a person can do. I enjoy every missionary, activity and meeting. I love to plan get-togethers and be with our missionaries when they visit, I love to hear their stories, I love to introduce parishioners to missionaries and the joys of missions, and I love to plan and go on mission trips!" Such personal enthusiasm and hands-on experience with mission is flourishing among Episcopalians and Anglicans in North America and Britain. A resurgence of interest in world mission among parishes and dioceses since 1975 has generated grassroots involvement, contributed to the spiritual, physical, educational, and economic lives of companions around the world, and transformed countless people at home.

The center of gravity for mission has shifted from national centers and organizations alone to shared initiatives between local communities and church-wide agencies. All Angels' Church in Manhattan, where Louisa Turner is a member, is a mid-sized parish that has helped support eight missionaries in such diverse areas as Nepal, Eastern Europe, Mexico, and India, fielded three short-term mission teams to South Africa and Appalachia, and worked with local international students. Many dioceses have developed major world mission commitments. The Diocese of Oklahoma, for instance, began a companionship with Uganda's Diocese of West Ankole in 1982 that undertakes substantial projects in education, healthcare, youth work, and post-war reconstruction through the Volunteer Oklahoma Outreach Mission (VOOM is the acronym!). Meanwhile, centralized mission programs are very active, whether in Britain, Canada, or the United States, alongside the many voluntary societies that specialize in particular kinds of mission.

How can a parish get involved in world mission? How can church members become more aware of what is happening religiously on the global scene? What can a diocese do to lift its people's eyes to the wider horizon of the global community and nurture opportunities for its parishes? How does one work with the many organizations that support and carry out mission around the world? How can a parish or diocese collaborate with agencies at church-wide headquarters that seek to catalyze world mission in the congregations? These are questions this chapter is designed to address. Having wrestled with issues of scripture, history, theology, religions, cultures, and vision, we now explore how church members can mobilize for mission in parish and diocesan communities.

～ Energizing Parishes for World Mission

The local congregation is the primary community in which Episcopalians and Anglicans, like most Christians, worship, celebrate, study, and minister with others. Parishes are central. People promoting diocesan and church-wide initiatives are often asked, quite properly: "That sounds good, but how will it work in the parishes? Have you tested this plan in any congregations? If not, why not?" We know that if something happens in a parish, then it is really happening, and we tend to be skeptical of ideas "dreamed up on high."

Pursuing mission with those whom you see from Sunday to Sunday is exciting because you share a daily or at least weekly life with them in the wider community of town, suburb, and city. You see each other in supermarkets and schools, or you may commute together. From newspapers, television, radio, and the Internet you gain an awareness of local events that offer opportunities to explore, like a visitor from another part of the world or a need elsewhere to which your community is especially sensitive. Every missionary I know has a congregation to nurture and support his or her call, for it is the vision and work of the local parish that raises up global missionaries by creating an environment in which God's call to the wider world can be heard. Moreover, the mission initiatives of diocese and autonomous province depend on the committed involvement of parishes. So when you begin by networking in your congregation, you are starting in the right place.

How might you go about catalyzing world mission work in your congregation? Here are some specific suggestions.

Talk with people who might share a global concern. Presumably you have chosen to be in a parish so that you do not have to live out your Christian life alone. That applies to your global discipleship as well, so seek out people who might like to explore world mission with you. Talking with your parish clergy will elicit both their support and the names of individuals to approach. People from other parts of the world who have settled in your midst are often delighted when "native" parishioners express interest in the concerns of other countries. People who have professional commitments in education, health, or business in other countries may wonder what is going on religiously where they work. They are excited to broaden their engagement there, and the international expertise they bring from their vocations is invaluable to any mission you do together. Individuals who grew up abroad often have a yen for the wider world that they want to develop. And even those who have no global background or expertise can bring a joyful enthusiasm that springs simply from their conviction that God is up to something out there in the world— and they want to be part of it!

Form a world mission activist group. When you have five to eight interested people, someone should convene the group to discuss first steps. Look for diversity—a good mix of nationalities, ages, races, gifts, and temperaments will help ensure that prayer happens as well as fundraising, good administration as well as hand-holding. At your first gathering you will want to share backgrounds and experiences, interests and particular enthusiasms. It is helpful to agree on a chairperson or co-chairs, choose a name for the group, and establish your meeting pattern (monthly is usually best).

Pray, ponder scripture, and learn about mission. Mission activists, like other activists, want to get about doing something immediately, but try to ensure that the group keeps growing in prayer, biblical awareness, and knowledge of new developments in mission. A devotional time at the beginning of each meeting helps the members be available to God and one another. Daily Devotions for Individuals and Families (BCP 136-140) or a similar brief outline can help structure your worship. Mission depends on prayer, so take time to pray for discernment and to intercede for particular missioners and projects, supplementing your concerns with the *Anglican Cycle of Prayer*, an intercession book published for the entire Anglican Communion. Discussing a scripture passage freshens your encounter with God's movement in mission and releases new insight and energy for the work. Share articles, books, or news stories of mission encounters that come to your attention.

Analyze the symbiosis between community and mission in your parish. Mission needs community to support it, and community needs mission to direct it. Community without mission dies out, and mission without community burns out. We need to ask, "We have wonderful parish life, but what fruit is it bearing in mission?" This is also a survival question: communities focused on themselves rather than on the world decline as their members realize that God's call is not being heeded. So take an inventory of the balance between community and mission in your parish. If there is no global vision, do your local outreaches have global connections that can be developed? If you already have global work, how can it be more integrated in the life of the parish?

Build on what is already happening. In every parish there is *some* hint of concern for the wider world on which to build—though it may seem a slender reed indeed! For example, your community probably takes collections for Episcopal Relief and Development

(USA), the Primate's Fund for World Relief (Canada), Christian Care (UK), or the United Thank Offering (USA). Just showing the videos from these funds and discussing their annual reports can help you increase awareness. Every Episcopalian is automatically a member of the Domestic and Foreign Missionary Society and so may be interested in letters from missionaries that you can download from the Mission Personnel area of the Episcopal Church's website. Someone may know of a missionary or agency staff person whom you could invite to speak. This is especially possible in the Church of England, where the networks of the Church Mission Society and the United Society for the Propagation of the Gospel over a more limited geography make speakers very accessible. A parishioner's interest in a particular country or the group's interest in a particular type of work may be a good starting place. Take an inventory of the various ties you already have, and begin building on those.

Offer mission education for all ages. Mission education will enable your community to work knowledgeably, stay alert for new possibilities, and avoid mistakes often made by mission activists. Offering occasional Sunday and midweek forums on aspects of mission and world Christianity will gradually build understanding about the history, theology, and practice of Christian mission. Include children and youth in your planning. For Episcopalians, the annual Church School Missionary Offering is ideal for teaching young children about mission with a specific church somewhere else in the world. Education is often most effective when it goes hand-in-hand with action. For the youth at St. Peter's in Cambridge, a school project on AIDS in Africa stimulated them to organize a fundraiser for children at a particular orphanage in Zimbabwe, through which, in turn, they learned about the work of churches in responding to the AIDS crisis. People want to learn about those with whom they are being drawn into companionship, and there are abundant resources you can use to broaden the horizon of their awareness.

Make connections with other communities and agencies. With grassroots interest growing and mission agencies proliferating, no parish needs to reinvent the mission wheel. Instead, look around you and make connections. Find out whether neighboring parishes need help with their existing mission commitments. Your deanery, district, or convocation may have projects underway that are virtually invisible until you ask about them, when it turns out the coordinators are longing for more participation. Many dioceses have world mission committees eager to help parishes mobilize. Church-wide headquarters in the United States, Canada, and Britain have materials they can send and lots more that you can access from websites, as do the various voluntary societies. As always, the most helpful connections are person-to-person, so try to talk or meet with key leaders who can assist you in your areas of concern. To help you find your way, in Britain contact the Partnership for World Mission; in Canada, the Volunteers in Mission Committee of General Synod; in the United States, the Episcopal Partnership for Global Mission.

Start small, and be open to growing. Mission affects the lives of people, so it is important to do a few things well rather than be half-hearted about many things. Let your first effort be something small and doable, like organizing a Saturday morning workshop, holding a fundraiser for one project, or inviting a mission speaker. Assess the event afterward and see what the group can learn for future events. Follow up on the leads that develop, see where they take you, and do not be afraid if they develop into major undertakings. Someone may feel called to Turkestan, or a group may want to organize a short-term mission to Guatemala, or a family may feel called to host an international refugee. God is probably at work in such developments, and you will find that the wider church has resources of information, coordination, and fundraising to help you support such ventures.

Highlight world mission in your worship. Liturgy is the primary way in which your community enacts corporately its life with God, so it is important that mission be prominent in your worship. Many congregations offer up by name the provinces and dioceses whose needs appear day by day in the *Anglican Cycle of Prayer.* Highlight in the prayers of intercession particular missionaries and projects that your community supports. Anthologies of prayers from around the world are a good source for specific prayers composed by Christians in other places. Arrange for scripture readings to be read in the different languages spoken by members of your community. Incorporate hymns and service music from other parts of the world. Iinvite missionaries to preach at your services. When you send out an individual or a team on mission, commission them in the liturgy so that they go with the community's prayer and care. Similarly, when missioners from another part of the world come to you, receive them with prayer in the midst of your worship. In these ways you can ensure that your mission and your worship enhance each other. As it happens, worship is also the most effective vehicle for publicizing what you do in global mission!

~ Energizing Dioceses for World Mission

Catalyzing mission initiatives in a diocese depends on many of the same strategies as in a parish, applied to the larger community. Talk with people who might share a global concern; in consultation with the bishop, form a world mission activist group; pray, ponder scripture, and learn about mission together; analyze the symbiosis between community and mission in your diocese; build on what is already happening in the parishes; make connections with other dioceses and agencies; start small, and be open to growing; highlight world mission in your diocesan worship life. Helpful resources are available from the Global Episcopal Mission Network, an association of dioceses engaged in world mission.

Since the 1970s, the creation of companion diocese relationships has done more than anything else to stimulate grassroots mission throughout the Anglican Communion. The excitement of knowing Christians in another country, the joy of growing in faith across cultural differences, the desire to help partners who may be in need—these prospects are drawing Anglicans into relationships and practical engagements far beyond their local areas. Lutherans have developed a similar pattern of companion synods. So a companion diocese relationship is an especially good place to start. It is crucial that the bishop be enthusiastically committed and that the diocese as a whole rally behind it, preferably through a resolution passed by convention or synod. Ordinarily, a relationship continues for two three-year terms, but a number of links have continued longer. The particular suggestions that follow here apply both to formal companionships and to diocesan global work in general.

Focus on companionships with people. Building relationships in community is the heart of mission, so diocesan strategy should focus primarily on companionships between people in the home diocese and people in the partner diocese. If you are in a diocese in a North Atlantic country, you will feel keenly the needs of fellow Christians in the Two-Thirds World, whether abuse of women or inadequate schools, neglected street children or the AIDS pandemic. The needs will channel your energy, but the relationships you build around addressing those needs will be the joy and life of the mission. With their substantial resources and institutional infrastructure, dioceses are often asked to contribute money to projects in other parts of the world. This is often appropriate, but a major opportunity is missed if funds are given without forming relationships. Ask yourselves, "How can we build enduring love around this need? How can we gather faces around this gift?" Reporting on a companionship tour of the Diocese of West Ankole in Uganda, Willis Jenkins of Oklahoma wrote:

> The spiritual impact American friendship has upon a parish is nearly tangible; it's in their smiles and sincerity of voice upon mention of Oklahoma. Pictures and letters are most appreciated, even more than money. . . . The relational emphasis of the Oklahoma-West Ankole link is often pointed out with appreciation and approval, even though the monetary aid of VOOM is relatively very small.[1]

Live and work in mutuality. One of the four covenants framed by the organizations of the Episcopal Partnership for Global Mission states that mission organizations must first receive the "invitation/permission from the relevant Anglican ecclesiastical authority, before engaging in a program or sending persons into an area where an Anglican body exists."[2] This guideline is meant to ensure that all mission initiatives are shared. Any mature human relationship is a mutual one, with both members contributing to and having their needs met in the relationship. This holds equally true of a companion diocese relationship. Each side in the companionship needs to give and receive, though the kinds of things given and received by each may differ. Unequal financial resources can distort the relationship's mutuality if money becomes a focus and other kinds of gifts are not recognized. Similarly, there needs to be balance in the sending and receiving of personnel, so that "their" people come to us in about the same numbers as "our" people go to them. The integrity of each party in the relationship must be respected. This means that neither side can set a ministry agenda for the other, but each side collaborates in carrying out the agenda the other has set for itself. At the same time, a mature relationship must include the possibility of making suggestions to the other party, and this is an important ministry if new gospel insights are to be realized. Such prayerful consultation may be important on issues of justice and peace or, say, in situations where a particular kind of evangelism is needed.

Stimulate parish involvement in mission. One of the main functions of a diocesan mission group is to catalyze global engagement by the parishes, for many congregations have few resources of experience or personnel on whom to draw. Simply asking every parish to identify its mission group reminds everyone to mobilize for outreach beyond their own community. Offering a half-day or evening workshop on how to form and nurture a global mission committee can be useful. World Mission Sunday, held every year throughout the church on the Last Sunday after the

Epiphany, is an excellent opportunity to provide parishes with educational materials on world mission, circulate a list of possible speakers, and gather support for diocese-wide initiatives. Central within any companion diocese relationship should be parish-to-parish companionships, for here parishioners can form friendships through letters and visits and develop a hands-on commitment to another Christian community. Such relationships require careful planning and nurture to maintain momentum in building relationship and to avoid creating unrealistic expectations on either side.

Become a diocese that sends and receives missionaries. This may seem like a tall order, but it is a reality in a number of dioceses. In the Diocese of Massachusetts, for instance, in ten years the Volunteers for Mission Committee helped send over sixty people on mission in Africa, Asia, Latin America, and Europe. Many of these were short-term assignments not needing church-wide appointment: youth on summer missions to Latin America, clergy to lead conferences or teach seminary courses in Africa, doctors and nurses to offer medical care in Haiti. Others were long-term assignments through agencies, mostly the Domestic and Foreign Missionary Society but also groups such as the South American Missionary Society and Anglican Frontier Missions. Operating on a limited budget, the diocesan group's modest grants serve as an endorsement that helps missioners raise support from individuals, parishes, and other groups. For individuals considering a call, the committee assists with discernment, conducts an application process, connects inquirers with relevant experts, and offers liaison with specific sending agencies. For agencies, a diocesan group is a helpful resource for screening and counsel. Long-term missionaries find it invaluable to be supported by three concentric circles of discernment: parish, diocese, and mission agency. Equally important, a diocesan mission personnel group needs to promote the receiving of missionaries from other parts of the world, individuals who can offer ministries that will benefit specific communities or the diocese as a whole.

Encourage all ages in mission. The increasingly popular youth mission trips build mission awareness and commitment into future leaders of the church. Just as children and youth must be included in mission education, world mission is a remarkable experience for children in families who minister in other cultures. "Why send a family of six to Africa when the same money could send two or three single missionaries?" one church leader exclaimed before Jane and I went with our four young children to Zimbabwe. He could not have been more mistaken. Being a family made us credible in family-centered Shona society, and it multiplied our relationships exponentially. The children's experience of African Christianity later drew them into commitments abroad and at home that affected American friends and their own vocations. Moving abroad with children has important familial and educational implications that must be considered seriously by prospective missionaries and their support groups, but it is a viable option that offers important gifts. Many young college students and graduates have a keen interest in serving abroad, and sponsoring them in mission helps their vocational discernment and often makes them mission enthusiasts for life. Increasing numbers of missioners are "finishers," people who have recently retired from their professions and wish to serve God abroad while their health is still strong. They bring maturity and breadth of experience, their highly developed skills make them very useful in host dioceses, and their retirement income offers them freedom of movement.

Ensure cross-cultural orientation and language training for missionaries. Research in the United States suggests that a geographic move is one of the most stressful life events, alongside divorce and the death of a loved one. Such stress is magnified when the move is across the world to an entirely different cultural and linguistic group. Intentional orientation is crucial to help prospective missionaries reflect on their mission theology, deepen their cultural sensitivity, consider dimensions of poverty and justice, and think about personal issues of finance, aging parents, children's education, healthcare, spousal roles, and the like. Such training is standard for personnel sponsored through a mission agency, and it is important to connect others with established programs. People going for a year or more should also undertake language training and should not be deterred by the frequent refrain, "Oh, you can get by because so many people know English." Regardless how many people know English, "getting by" is not the stuff of mission. Knowing the local language is crucial to what mission is really about: understanding a culture, building relationships, offering solidarity, living as companions.

Be flexible with different expressions of authority. Members of Christian denominations trying to work with their counterparts on a different continent are sometimes startled by how differently authority is expressed through structures and offices that look similar. Anglicans and Lutherans in the countries of the North Atlantic, for instance, have bishops, but lay people and clergy often are free to take initiative through a commission or committee. Expecting to interact with a similarly empowered group in another part of the world, they may feel frustrated when their communications are always routed to the partner's bishop and the reply, when it comes, is addressed not to themselves but to their bishop. That is not the time to campaign for democracy in the church! Recognize, instead, that similar structures have developed differently in different places and that mission can flourish as each side works with the other *as the other is*. As we learn from one another, a diocese in the Global North may ensure that its bishop is truly engaged and a bishop in the Global South may convene a committee to assist in the relationship.

Affirm theological diversity in mission thinking. Anglican dioceses are generally large and diverse enough for there to be considerable variation in people's thinking about mission, and this is true of Lutheran synods as well. Some, for example, might see evangelism as central in mission while others feel that preventing AIDS, empowering women, or protecting children is crucial. People may differ with one another about the centrality of Christ or the status of other religions. Realizing that theological diversity is inevitable in diocesan life, we must welcome all perspectives to the mission planning table. Especially inevitable is theological diversity among communities in different parts of the world. If we share Paul's conviction that the body of Christ is diverse in its gifts, we will provide opportunities for different visions of mission to be expressed. Out of the experience of living with such diversity among themselves, the member organizations of the Episcopal Partnership for Global Mission agreed to this covenant: "Desiring to avoid untested assumptions about one another, we will seek to understand our various mission theologies by committing time and resources to listen and talk together with honesty and mutual respect."[3] That is a good covenant also for individuals within dioceses and for all in companion diocese relationships.

∽ Mission in a World of Inequality

The theme of tension between wealth and poverty has recurred often in this book. It is important in our polarized world that we consider it once again as applied to actual mission encounters, whether those of individual missionaries, short-term teams, or even the fact-finding and orientation trips undertaken by mission committees.

A letter from Ellen Hargrave, who with her husband Bob ministers in Kenya through Africa Inland Mission, expresses the anguish many feel in offering witness as privileged Christians in the midst of poverty:

> I am realizing today just how privileged we are.... Today, another woman who I never met stopped in. She said that Rosemary had helped her in the past and where was Rosemary. I informed her that Rosemary had moved to England and wasn't coming back. She then questioned me, "What am I to do?" Her child had been hospitalized and the bill was the equivalent of about $100. Now that would be a very minor hospital bill for any of our families. But that is pretty big for people living on the edge waiting for rain.... Yet, we really can't afford to pay everyone's hospital bill that comes to our door. Or their school fees. Or feed their families. One feels so frustrated.... Are we to be like Sister Teresa and live like the poorest of the poor ourselves? Do we subsist on a bit of rice each day? Then we have more to give the poor ourselves? But then, what about our children? Is it right for us to sit here with our fridge and

pantry full of food deciding just what will we
have for our next meal while others are hungry
around us? Will these dilemmas never cease?
Please pray for us as we attempt to live for
Christ in a needy world.[4]

Missionaries are often intensely aware of the dispari-
ty between what they have and what others do not.
Through their efforts in agricultural development the
Hargraves are working to make a regional economy
self-sufficient, but they feel empathy for individuals
in crisis and would like to help everyone. Another
missionary's past commitment to helping a particular
person increases the pressure in this case. Yet trying to
solve each individual problem would threaten their
presence there, especially if it were to diminish their
ability to provide adequately for their own children.

Juxtapositions of affluence and poverty make people uncomfortable, and rightly so, for they raise a
host of questions about injustice and redistribution,
subsistence and excess, greed and generosity, compassion and indifference. Such discomfort prompts many
in the Global North to hesitate about considering mission service or traveling to other parts of the world.
Sometimes the discomfort prompts criticism of those
who do serve among the poor. "They have a car,"
someone might comment, "and right in their neighborhood children are going to bed hungry!" "Living at
the same level as the people" is often held up as the
ideal lifestyle for missionaries in poor areas of the
world, and living otherwise may be considered selfish
and callous.

Missionaries are called to lifestyles that nurture
companionship and do not emphasize the greater
resources they may have, and the vast majority of
missionaries are faithful to this call. However, to

expect missionaries to "live at the same level" as, for instance, the 1.5 billion people who are desperately poor is misguided and may express a lack of awareness of actual working situations. Virtually every society has a wide spectrum of economic lifestyles, and most missionaries interact daily with people in a variety of economic strata, just as they would in their home countries. Their compensation is usually comparable to that of a local school teacher, not to that of the business executives and institutional leaders with whom they also rub shoulders.

The expectation of poverty is also not one that people in the *receiving* culture affirm. When they arrived as missionaries in Madagascar, Todd and Patsy McGregor wanted to live with the people and at the people's level. So they and their two children shared a house with two Malagasy families. In the midst of cultural adjustment, settling the children and getting their work underway, they realized at the end of the first year that their family life was in tatters. At that point, the Malagasy bishop exclaimed, "We don't *want* you to be poor like us!" That was a clarifying comment. Poverty distorts life, which is why God decries it throughout scripture. Solidarity is crucial, but it does not entail trying to be just the same as the people to whom one goes. They *know* you are not just the same, so the attempt to appear so is sheer pretense. What people appreciate is that you are *there with them* even though you *are* different in many ways: nationally, ethnically, and, yes, economically.

The expectation that missionaries be poor may conceal an unconscious assumption that economic disparities are fine in our world, just so long as the rich and the poor do not have to see each other. Is there a difference between a missionary living in a middle-class house in São Paulo and any other

Christian living in a middle-class house in Ottawa, Miami, or Liverpool? No, for in each case the poor whom Jesus blessed are equally close at hand, although more numerous in São Paulo. Since one can justifiably cast the Global North as rich and the Global South as poor, missionaries from the north are sometimes asked, "How can you live so close to such poverty?" Well, the poverty is still very much there, even if you do *not* live close to it. At stake is whether Christians will promote the isolation that allows indifference to flourish or will build solidarity in a global community. Solidarity means being there, not supposing that the poverty is somehow less urgent, less painful simply because you do not see it from thousands of miles away. Life in the global village means, among other things, recognizing that the poverty of Bombay is just as close, just as outrageous, whether one is in Los Angeles or in Bombay itself. Being there does not mean you can eradicate the poverty or reverse the injustice, nor that you will never make mistakes, but it does offer a sacrament of Christ's solidarity with those who suffer. When we are far from the world's catastrophically poor, that is when we need to turn Ellen Hargrave's prayer request into a request for *ourselves:* "Please pray for us as we attempt to live for Christ in a needy world." Being faithful is harder at a distance than it is up close.

～ The Pilgrimage of Mission
A pilgrim is one who journeys in search of God. Clearly, a person searching for God already knows God in some very important ways, so the pilgrim is one who seeks a deeper knowledge of God, a broader experience of God, a more intimate relationship with God. A pilgrim is someone who has heard and heeded the admonition "Your God is too small."

At the heart of authentic mission is the pilgrim impulse, the intuition that our vision of God will be clarified, our thought about God verified, and our life with God energized through companionship with the other—other peoples, other cultures, other languages, other histories. In the course of sharing the gospel with a group of Masai in Tanzania, American Roman Catholic missionary Vincent Donovan encouraged his listeners to search out the High God in the midst of their Masai-defined views of the divine. One of the Masai asked him, "Has your tribe found the High God? Have you known him?" Remembering how Europeans and Americans have often reduced God to a tribal and nationalist deity, Donovan replied,

> No, *we have not* found the High God. My tribe has not known him. For us, too, he is the unknown God. But we are searching for him. I have come a long, long distance to invite you to search for him with us. Let us search for him together. Maybe, together, we will find him.[5]

Such humility undergirded Donovan's remarkable ministry of helping the Masai develop a Masai understanding of Christ and a Masai form of church life. Evangelizing a people who had never heard the gospel, Donovan felt that he himself was rediscovering Christianity.

Authentic mission is a paradox. We have good news to share, the news of what God has done through Christ in the power of the Holy Spirit. What that news truly means, however, we discover along the way as we share it in love. Meeting the other, we glimpse what God is really up to in the world. Going with a gospel, we discover the gospel. Venturing as Christians, we begin to become Christians. So it is that authentic mission is a pilgrimage that transforms the missionary.

"I was just amazed. It shocked me!" said fifteen-year-old Romeo Mack of Boston's South End after a pilgrimage to the Bernard Mizeki Festival in 1996. "I was around a lot of youth in Zimbabwe. We'd just be hanging out, and they'd be talking about *God*. That was a major thing, because where I live, people don't usually talk about God, like they try to stay away from church, like it's a bad thing." Mack was one of sixty participants in what was probably the first self-professed pilgrimage by western Christians to a Christian community in sub-Saharan Africa. What difference did it make to him? He wanted to share the news with his friends back home: "I want to bring them the fact that if you go to Africa you see people rejoicing about God, in church, outside of church, in their homes, in their schools, on the streets. So I'm going to try to lean over towards that way and hope that my friends lean toward God more."[6]

The explosive vitality of Christianity in the Global South highlights the pilgrim motif for many who go on mission from the Global North. The short-term missions undertaken by parishes and dioceses will benefit from being reconceived as pilgrimages to vibrant Christian communities in the Two-Thirds World, Christianity's new center of gravity. Churches and schools may still get built and painted by visiting teams, but organizers will focus more on experiencing the worship and ministry of the communities to whom they go. Orientation to economic justice issues prompts short-term mission pilgrims to develop responsible lifestyles and undertake political advocacy when they return home. Vocational discernment should be an undergirding purpose in all short-term missions as pilgrims ask themselves, "How is God calling me through this experience to change the way I live? What is God calling me to do with my life?"

Anglican missionary numbers are on the rise as new agencies grow and entire churches become more engaged. Shifting from static low levels, the Episcopal Church's Domestic and Foreign Missionary Society's sending work grew to over one hundred volunteers and appointees abroad during the millennial year, and the total from Episcopal agencies in general exceeded two hundred, with several thousand on short-term teams. The Church of Nigeria Missionary Society, founded in 1997, now has eleven missionaries, and innovative approaches are emerging for sending and receiving. Concerned for the 1.7 billion people in the world who have not heard the gospel, Anglican Frontier Missions is partnering with Nigerian dioceses to support Nigerian evangelists working with previously unreached groups in Cameroon, Mali, Chad, Benin, and Niger. As mission companions serve as sacraments of Christ's universal invitation and solidarity abroad, they also serve as sacraments for the church at home. Their lives indelibly marked by pilgrimage with mission companions in very different places, they bring tidings of the church "out there." Through them the church at home becomes a pilgrim church, growing through a global community of discipleship. Missionaries from the Global South will soon, we pray, be a major phenomenon in the Global North, for northern societies need gospel insight and power from the south, whether in fresh evangelization or in building up existing churches.

Mission is not primarily a mandate, theory, or strategy. It is rather a joyful journey with God, a journey whose destination is always just beyond the horizon, a journey where all we know of the outcome is that we will know more of God, more of God, more of

God. I close this book, therefore, simply with reflections by people who have made that pilgrimage central in their lives, whether for short periods or long.

Fresh out of college, Bryan Kane worked with
Sudanese refugees for two years in Cairo, after which
he reflected:

> There is a continued temptation to think that I
> have made no real difference; that poverty is
> only increasing; and that the end result of two
> years of hard work is only more problems. One
> thing that Jesus continued to teach me in Cairo
> was that I am not the Messiah. *He* is.... In leav-
> ing, I have had to continue to give everything
> over to the Lord in prayer, trusting him not
> only for the people and work that I am leaving
> behind, but also for that which lies ahead.[7]

In over forty years as missionaries in Liberia and
Lesotho, Judy and John Gay developed the depth and
breadth of perspective that comes with lifetime commitment. Nearing retirement, they wrote:

> Our problem is that we have found niches in the
> large enterprise of helping Africans cope with
> the overpowering presence of a global economy
> and culture. We must now move out of those
> niches, and with God's help give positive
> encouragement to our friends here to do the
> work we have been doing. We are very definite-
> ly dispensable, but the jobs we have been doing
> are indispensable, and so our task in our final
> year is to make sure that there is no break when
> we go. Ideally, no one should notice when we
> pack our goods, lock our door, turn over the
> keys to our colleagues, and retire. Please pray

for us that we can depart in a quiet and good way, confident that the work will continue.[8]

The mission pilgrimage can be difficult in ways that push one to realize, over and over again, that God is the missionary on whom all our work must depend. Coordinating a variety of mission companionships in Haiti, the western hemisphere's poorest country, P. J. Woodall wrote:

> Sometimes it seems almost hopeless that any-thing will ever be better for the people of Haiti. The political situation is very discouraging. I think that all the different people of God work-ing in Haiti bring the only hope that there is for this country. I can remember times in our lives when I just could not figure out a solution to a predicament. I would struggle and struggle; it was just beyond my ability to take care of the problem. And so, as a last resort I would finally turn it over to God and God would work it out. This is how I feel about Haiti. It will take turn-ing it over to God. God is the only one who can possibly make this a better place. It is beyond human abilities without God's help.[9]

The mission pilgrim serves as a sacrament of Christ's solidarity. Yet how is the pilgrim nourished for the journey? Perhaps by receiving the entire expe-rience as a sacrament of Christ. From the Diocese of Tabora in Tanzania, missionaries Terry and Judy Laduke wrote:

> Life here is good. Amidst phenomenal difficul-ties, life is good. This is a place of extremes. People are incredibly poor yet rich beyond meas-ure. Our hearts ache with compassion but burst with joy. We are surrounded by huge expanses

of sky, dry grass and mango trees—apparently empty, but even the trees have eyes and ears. There is no such thing as privacy. We live on a small island of Christianity surrounded by a sea of Islam. Feeling young but treated like an elderly person (life expectancy is 50 years). Humbled by love, appalled by graft. Carrying buckets of water to be strained, boiled and filtered and then put in a fridge. Sharing half a banana with the ever so entertaining neighborhood monkey and turning around to face hungry children. It is difficult to explain, but life is good. God is good.[10]

God's goodness—that is the final horizon of mission, and it is sufficient.

Endnotes

∾ **Chapter 1: Dilemma and Discernment in Mission Today**

1. Frank T. Griswold, "Some Reflections on Becoming a People of Jubilee," typed circular (15 June 1999): 2.

2. "Partners in Mission," the website of the Anglican Church of Canada: www.anglican.ca/synod98/reports/r-pim.htm.

3. Eleanor Johnson and John Clark, eds., *Anglicans in Mission: A Transforming Journey: Report of Missio, the Mission Commission of the Anglican Communion, to the Anglican Consultative Council, meeting in Edinburgh, Scotland, September 1999* (London: SPCK, 2000), 44-45.

4. Resolution II.1b.ii, in *The Official Report of the Lambeth Conference 1998* (Harrisburg: Morehouse, 1999), 388.

5. Daniel Johnson Fleming, "If Buddhists Came to Our Town," *Christian Century* 46.9 (28 February 1929): 293-294.

6. David B. Barrett, George T. Kurian, and Todd M. Johnson, *World Christian Encyclopedia: A Comparative Survey of Churches and Religions in the Modern World*, 2nd edition, vol. 1 (New York: Oxford University Press, 2001), 772, 785.

7. *World Christian Encyclopedia,* 4, 13-15.

⮜ Chapter 2: The Missionary God in Scripture
1. The distinction between centripetal mission in the Old Testament and centrifugal mission the New Testament is suggested by Johannes Blauw, *The Missionary Nature of the Church: A Survey of the Biblical Theology of Mission* (New York: McGraw-Hill, 1962), 54, 66.

⮜ Chapter 3: Mission in History
1. George E. P. Broderick, *History of the Diocese of Southern Rhodesia (formerly the Diocese of Mashonaland)* (typed manuscript, 1953; Zimbabwe National Archives), 269-273.
2. George Wyndham Hamilton Knight-Bruce, *Journals of the Mashonaland Mission, 1888 to 1892* (London: Society for the Propagation of the Gospel in Foreign Parts, 1892), 9.
3. George Wyndham Hamilton Knight-Bruce, *Memories of Mashonaland* (London and New York: Edward Arnold, 1895), 43.
4. Tertullian, *Apology* 39.7, trans. T. R. Glover, Loeb Classical Library (Cambridge: Harvard University Press, 1984), 177.
5. David B. Barrett, ed., *World Christian Encyclopedia: A Comparative Study of Churches and Religions in the Modern World,* A.D. *1900-2000* (Nairobi: Oxford University Press, 1982), 23-24.
6. Bede, *Ecclesiastical History of the English People* [I.30], ed. Bertram Colgrave and R. A. B. Mynors (Oxford: Clarendon Press, 1969), 106-109.
7. Paul Tillich, *Theology of Culture*, ed. Robert C. Kimball (London, Oxford, and New York: Oxford University Press, 1959), 42.

8. William Carey, *An Enquiry into the Obligations of Christians to Use Means for the Conversion of the Heathen* (first published 1792; London: Carey Kingsgate Press, 1961), 63.

9. Stephen Neill, *A History of Christian Missions* (Baltimore: Penguin, 1984),153.

10. Neill, *History*, 156-157.

11. Neill, *History*, 68-69.

12. Neill, *History*, 97-98.

13. Neill, *History*, 121.

14. Bartolomé de Las Casas, *History of the Indies* (c. 1540), quoted in H. McKennie Goodpasture, ed., *Cross and Sword: An Eyewitness History of Christianity in Latin America* (Maryknoll: Orbis, 1989), 11.

15. Douglas Steere, *God's Irregular: Arthur Shearly Cripps: A Rhodesian Epic* (London: SPCK, 1973), 94, 34-35.

∽ Chapter 4: The Anglican and Episcopal Mission Story

1. John Sentamu, "Tribalism, Religion and Despotism in Uganda: Archbishop Janani Luwum," in Andrew Chandler, ed., *The Terrible Alternative: Christian Martyrdom in the Twentieth Century* (London and New York: Cassell, 1998), 153.

2. Justinian Welz, *A Christian and Sincere Admonition to All Orthodox Christians of the Augsburg Confession Concerning a Special Society through which with the Help of God Our Evangelical Religion may be Spread*, in James A. Scherer, *Justinian Welz: Essays by an Early Prophet of Mission* (Grand Rapids: Eerdmans, 1969), 59.

3. Max Warren, ed., *To Apply the Gospel: Selections from the Writings of Henry Venn* (Grand Rapids: William B. Eerdmans, 1971), 63.

4. James Thayer Addison, *The Episcopal Church in the United States, 1789-1931* (New York: Charles Scribner's Sons, 1951), 74.

5. "Constitution of the Domestic and Foreign Missionary Society," in *Journal of the Proceedings of the Bishops, Clergy, and Laity of the Protestant Episcopal Church in the United States of America in General Convention* (New York: Protestant Episcopal Press, 1835), 129.

6. Walter Herbert Stowe, "A Turning Point—General Convention of 1835," *Historical Magazine of the Protestant Episcopal Church* 4 (September 1935): 176.

7. "Constitution of the DFMS," in *Journal*, 131.

8. Stowe, "A Turning Point," in *Historical Magazine*, 171.

9. *The Proper for the Lesser Feasts and Fasts, 1997* (New York: Church Publishing, 1998), 388.

10. Ian Douglas, *Fling Out the Banner! The National Church Ideal and the Foreign Mission of the Episcopal Church* (New York: Church Hymnal Corporation, 1996).

11. Roland Allen, *Missionary Methods: St. Paul's or Ours?* (Grand Rapids: William B. Eerdmans, 1962).

12. William R. Hutchison, *Errand to the World: American Protestant Thought and Foreign Missions* (Chicago: University of Chicago Press, 1987), 176-177.

13. Douglas, *Fling Out the Banner!*, 173, 294-296.

14. "Mutual Responsibility and Interdependence in the Body of Christ," in Stephen F. Bayne, Jr., *Mutual Responsibility and Interdependence in the Body of Christ, with Related Background Documents* (New York: Seabury Press, 1963), 18, 21-22, 24.

15. Anglican Consultative Council, *Partners in Mission, Second Meeting: Dublin, Ireland, 17-27 July 1973*

(London: Society for Promoting Christian Knowledge, 1973), 53.

16. E. Stanley Jones, *Gandhi: Portrayal of a Friend* (Nashville: Abingdon, 1983), 110.

17. E. Stanley Jones, *The Christ of the Indian Road* (London: Hodder and Soughton, 1925), 146-148.

∿ Chapter 5: Christian Mission and Other Religions

1. Letter, William Bacon Stevens to Horatio Potter, 5 March 1877, in *Appeal to the Protestant Episcopal Churches of Massachusetts for Funds to Endow a Missionary College in China*, pamphlet.

2. Kenneth Cracknell, *Justice, Courtesy and Love: Theologians and Missionaries Encountering World Religions, 1846-1914* (London: Epworth Press, 1995), 191-206.

3. Frederick Denison Maurice, *The Religions of the World and their Relations to Christianity* (Boston: Gould and Lincoln, 1854), 32, 195-196, and throughout.

4. Raimundo Panikkar, *The Unknown Christ of Hinduism: Towards an Ecumenical Christophany*, rev. and enlarged edition (Maryknoll: Orbis, 1981), 169.

5. *Official Report of the Lambeth Conference 1998*, 138-147.

6. Frederick R. Wilson, *The San Antonio Report: Your Will be Done: Mission in Christ's Way* [Commission on World Mission and Evangelism, World Council of Churches] (Geneva: WCC Publications, 1990), 32.

7. David B. Barrett and Todd M. Johnson, "Annual Statistical Table on Global Mission: 2000," *International Bulletin of Missionary Research* 24.1 (January 2000): 24.

8. Lamin Sanneh, *Translating the Message: The Missionary Impact on Culture* (Maryknoll: Orbis, 1989), 1-8, 182-210.

~ **Chapter 6: Mission in Many Cultures**
1. J. Christy Wilson, Jr., ed., *Bringing Christ to All the World: Selections from the Writings of Dr. Adoniram Judson Gordon* (Hamilton, Mass.: Gordon-Conwell Printing Services, 1988), 63.
2. *Annual Report of the Domestic and Foreign Missionary Society of the Protestant Episcopal Church in the United States of America 1899*, 188-189, quoted in Douglas, *Fling Out the Banner!*, 94.
3. Daniel J. Fleming, *Whither Bound in Mission* (New York: Association Press, 1925), 1-22, 43-44.
4. Stephen Neill, *Colonialism and Christian Missions* (New York: McGraw-Hill, 1966), 413.
5. Allen, *Missionary Methods*, 142.
6. Jones, *Christ of the Indian Road*, 232.
7. Robert Shreiter, *Constructing Local Theologies* (Maryknoll: Orbis, 1985).
8. Max Warren, "General Introduction to the Christian Presence Series," in Kenneth Cragg, *Sandals at the Mosque: Christian Presence amid Islam* (London: SCM Press, 1959), 9-10.

~ **Chapter 7: A Vision for Mission in the Twenty-First Century**
1. Joan and Lou Mattia, missionary letter home, March 2000.
2. Nan Cobbey, "Nine Days Trapped," in "The Persecuted Church: Today's Martyrs Face Untold Terror," *Episcopal Life* (July-August 1997): 11.
3. Patricia Powers, "From the Mailbag" [reports from missionaries posted in the "Mission Personnel Notes"

section of the Anglican and Global Relations area of the Episcopal Church's website], November 1999.

4. Standing Commission on Evangelism, *Go Listen and Tell: The Presentation of Jesus Christ*, Report of the Standing Commission on Evangelism to the General Convention, Phoenix, 1991 (Cincinnati: Forward Movement, 1991), 7.

5. Johnson and Clark, *Anglicans in Mission*, 25. In this volume, note also "Five Marks of Mission," pp. 19-21; "Ten Priorities in Evangelism," pp. 121-125; and "Ten Principles of Partnership," pp. 126-129.

6. Division for Global Mission, Evangelical Lutheran Church in America, *Global Mission in the Twenty-first Century: A Vision of Evangelical Faithfulness in God's Mission* (Chicago: ELCA, 1997), 5-20.

7. Stewart Lane, "From the Mailbag," February 2000.

8. An instance is the AIDS initiative inaugurated in 2000 in the Anglican Diocese of Manicaland, Zimbabwe, called *Ukama*, the Shona word for "relationship" and also an acronym for United in Knowledge Against *Mukondombera* or AIDS.

9. Desmond Tutu, *No Future Without Forgiveness* (New York: Doubleday, 1999).

10. Sonja Hoekstra-Foss, "Letter from a Missionary: A Horror Returns in a Different Time," *Episcopal Life* (July-August 1999): 2.

11. Joan and Lou Mattia, missionary letter home, March 2000.

12. Tom and Barbara Lutton, "From the Mailbag," January 2000.

13. Standing Commission on World Mission, *The Primacy of Mission in the Church's Life* in *The Blue Book 2000: Reports of the Committees, Commissions, Boards and Agencies of the General Convention of the Episcopal Church: Seventy-Third General Convention, Denver,*

Colorado, July 2000 (New York: Church Publishing, 2000), 498-499.

14. Loren Mead, *The Once and Future Church: Reinventing the Congregation for a New Mission Frontier* (Washington, D. C.: Alban Institute, 1991).

15. *The Official Report of the Lambeth Conference 1998: Transformation and Renewal: July 18-August 9, 1998, Lambeth Palace; Canterbury, England* (Harrisburg: Morehouse, 1999), 145.

16. Phoebe Griswold, Address to Episcopal Relief and Development Luncheon, 2000 General Convention of the Episcopal Church, 7 July 2000.

∽ **Chapter 8: Energizing Communities for Mission**

1. Willis Jenkins, "Your Companion Parish," in "Report to the Board of the Volunteer Oklahoma Outreach Mission" (typescript, 1999), 2.

2. "Plan to Establish the Episcopal Partnership for Global Mission," in *The Blue Book 2000*, 503.

3. "Plan to Establish the Episcopal Partnership," in *The Blue Book 2000*, 503.

4. Ellen Hargrave, missionary letter home, April 2000.

5. Vincent Donovan, *Christianity Rediscovered* (Maryknoll: Orbis, 1982), 46.

6. Titus Presler, "From Boston to Zimbabwe: Young pilgrims find the heart of God," *Episcopal Life* (September 1996): 1, 3.

7. Bryan Kane, "From the Mailbag," October 1999.

8. John and Judy Gay, "From the Mailbag," February 2000.

9. P. J. Woodall, "From the Mailbag," December 1999.

10. Terry and Judy Laduke, "From the Mailbag," December 1999.

Resources

∾ Prayer and Worship

Prayer is central in world mission. Used throughout the Anglican Communion is the *Anglican Cycle of Prayer* (Forward Movement), a two-year booklet that cites the needs of a different diocese each day and includes maps and descriptions of each Anglican province. A bimonthly *Prayer Calendar* leaflet includes Episcopal missionaries serving with all agencies and is available from the Episcopal Church Missionary Community.

A number of prayer anthologies include contributions from around the world, one of which is *Prayers Encircling the World* (SPCK, 1998). Anthologies of songs are useful in worship, and the Episcopal hymnal supplement *Wonder, Love, and Praise* (Church Hymnal, 1997) includes hymns from the world church. As you communicate with companions in a particular part of the world, consider locating their prayer book and using it occasionally in your worship.

∾ Worldwide Web and Internet

The worldwide web offers instant access to immense amounts of information that a few years ago took weeks or months of correspondence to gather. Websites are established for mission-related organizations, many dioceses, and most Anglican provinces and ecumenical companions around the world. Sites also provide postal addresses, telephone numbers, and e-mail addresses. Good places to begin are the Anglican and Global Relations (AGR) area of the Episcopal Church website (www.episcopalchurch.org); the linked site of the Episcopal Partnership for Global Mission, which networks over fifty organizations (www.episcopalchurch.org/epgm); and the site of the Global Episcopal Mission Network, which includes over fifty dioceses (www.gemn.org).

Pertinent news is electronically accessible through the listserves Anglican Communion News Service and Episcopal News Service. MissionMobilizers is a listserve for information-sharing from every standpoint. "Moving picture" presentations of mission work have energized congregations since the days of silent movies, through the videotape era, and now into the frontier of digital video disks and electronic streaming. Mission organizations have ample resources and respond readily to inquiries.

Correspondence with church leaders around the world and with missionaries is accessible via e-mail as well as post. They will be glad to hear from you. At the same time, be aware that mission partners may have great demands on their time and energy, especially as they may struggle with logistical difficulties. Write letters that count! Missionaries regularly write general letters to friends and supporters, and they will be happy to add you to their electronic or postal mailing lists. Letters from missionaries are posted regularly on the websites of AGR and other mission agencies.

∿ Periodicals

Episcopal Life, the Episcopal Church's monthly magazine, features missionaries and covers mission concerns and celebrations in other parts of the world. The weekly *Church Times* in England offers a similar broad scope. *Anglican World*, published quarterly by the Anglican Communion Office in London, is a must for communion-wide developments. Particular mission agencies are happy to add you to their mailing lists.

Several international mission quarterlies publish articles that are both scholarly and accessible to a broader audience. *Missiology* focuses on issues in mission abroad and in support at home, while *International Bulletin of Missionary Research* concentrates on historical and theological issues. *The International Review of Mission* is published by the World Council of Churches and follows ecumenical discussions.

∿ Case Studies and Biographies

Case studies take group discussions of cultural encounters, interreligious issues, and mission management out of theory and into practice. Alan Neely's *Christian Mission: A Case Study Approach* (Orbis, 1995) includes contextual background and bibliographic resources for each case. Charles and Francis Hiebert's *Case Studies in Missions* (Baker, 1987) provides briefer cases that are self-explanatory.

Biographies inspire engagement with the personal dimension of mission and world Christianity. *The Biographical Dictionary of Christian Mission*, edited by Gerald Anderson (Eerdmans, 1998), is a useful reference. Here are several biographies I have found inspiring. *The Religious Revolution in the Ivory Coast: The Prophet Harris and the Harrist Church* by Sheila Walker (University of North Carolina, 1983) introduces

William Wadé Harris and the church he inspired in West Africa. Life stories of the twentieth-century martyrs who grace the west entrance of Westminster Abbey (cited in chapter four) are edited by Andrew Chandler in *The Terrible Alternative: Christian Martyrdom in the Twentieth Century* (Cassell, 1998). E. Stanley Jones's *Gandhi: Portrayal of a Friend* Abingdon, 1983) offers arresting insights into both Gandhi and Jones, one of the twentieth century's outstanding missionaries. Jean Farrant offers a full account of Central Africa's first Anglican missionary martyr in *Mashonaland Martyr: Bernard Mizeki and the Pioneer Church* (Oxford, 1966). *God's Irregular: Arthur Shearly Cripps: A Rhodesian Epic* by Douglas Steere (SPCK, 1973) discusses the British missionary who advocated for Africans in Rhodesia.

∽ History

The major resource for understanding statistically the range and diversity of world Christianity is *World Christian Encyclopedia: A Comparative Survey of Churches and Religions in the Modern World*, second edition, by David Barrett, George Kurian, and Todd Johnson (Oxford, 2001). This two-volume work provides population figures for religions and denominations, an overview of religious institutions, and the state of Christian outreach in every country of the world.

For a readable overview of twenty centuries of mission, Stephen Neill's classic *A History of Christian Missions* (Penguin, 1984) is the place to start. Church of England efforts are covered in the multi-author anniversary volumes about the two principal societies: *Three Centuries of Mission: The United Society for the Propagation of the Gospel, 1701-2000* by Daniel O'Connor and others (Continuum, 2000), and *The*

Church Mission Society and World Christianity, 1799-1999, edited by Kevin Ward and Brian Stanley (Eerdmans, 2000). Lamin Sanneh's compelling account of the role of translation in mission is *Translating the Message: The Missionary Impact on Culture* (Orbis, 1989).

For the Episcopal story in world mission, Ian Douglas's *Fling Out the Banner!: The National Church Ideal and the Foreign Mission of the Episcopal Church* (Church Publishing, 1996) is definitive. American Protestant mission is analyzed by William Hutchison in *Errand to the World: American Protestant Thought and Foreign Missions* (University of Chicago, 1987). Dana Robert explores the role of women in mission in *American Women in Mission: A Social History of Their Thought and Practice* (Mercer University, 1996). Mary Donovan details the mission story of Episcopal women in *A Different Call: Women's Ministries in the Episcopal Church, 1850-1920* (Morehouse-Barlow, 1986).

Current mission developments in the Anglican Communion are summarized in *Anglicans in Mission: A Transforming Journey* by Missio, the Mission Commission of the Anglican Communion, edited by Eleanor Johnson and John Clark (SPCK, 2000). The mission and interfaith recommendations of the most recent Lambeth Conference appear in *The Official Report of the Lambeth Conference 1998* (Morehouse, 1999). Practical proposals by current Episcopal practitioners are found in *New Wineskins for Global Mission*, edited by Sharon Stockdale (William Carey, 1996).

～ Bible and Theology

The standard overview of mission in the Bible is *The Biblical Foundations of Mission* by Donald Senior and

Carroll Stuhlmueller (Orbis, 1984). Kwok Pui-lan offers an Asian feminist perspective in *Discovering the Bible in the Non-Biblical World* (Orbis Books, 1995). John Koenig's *The Feast of the World's Redemption: Eucharistic Origins and Christian Mission* (Trinity, 2000) explores eucharist in the New Testament as a paradigm for mission.

The most comprehensive treatment of mission theology is David Bosch's *Transforming Mission: Paradigm Shifts in Theology of Mission* (Orbis, 1991). An accessible review of the twentieth century in the West is Timothy Yates's *Christian Mission in the Twentieth Century* (Cambridge University, 1994).

Hope and Justice for All in the Americas: Discerning God's Mission, edited by Oscar Bolioli (Friendship, 1998), summarizes a Latin American mission consultation sponsored by the National Council of Churches in Costa Rica. Gustavo Guttiérez's *A Theology of Liberation: History, Politics and Salvation* (Orbis, 1973) is the founding document of liberation theology. Influential in African mission theology are John Pobee's *Toward an African Theology* (Abingdon, 1979) and Kwesi Dickson's *Theology in Africa* (Orbis, 1984). Desmond Tutu stresses the centrality of reconciliation in *No Future Without Forgiveness* (Doubleday, 1999). Kosuke Koyama's *Waterbuffalo Theology* (Orbis, 1989) is an engaging view of mission in Asia. Anthony Gittins explores a sacramental view of mission in *Bread for the Journey: The Mission of Transformation and the Transformation of Mission* (Orbis, 1993).

Key documents appear in Norman Thomas's *Classic Texts in Mission and World Christianity* (Orbis, 1995). For major conciliar, Roman Catholic, Orthodox, and evangelical mission documents, consult *New Directions in Mission and Evangelism 1: Basic*

Statements 1974-1991, edited by James Scherer and Stephen Bevans (Orbis, 1992).

～ Religion and Culture

New developments in world Christianity ring changes in both religion and culture. *Christianity Rediscovered* (Orbis, 1982) offers a compelling vision arising from Vincent Donovan's work among the Masai in Tanzania. Titus Presler's *Transfigured Night: Mission and Culture in Zimbabwe's Vigil Movement* (University of South Africa, 1999) explores a gospel-culture inter-action that is energizing mission by Africans. *Quest for Belonging: Introduction to a Study of African Independent Churches* by Marthinus Daneel (Mambo, 1987) introduces African-initiated churches, as does *African Initiatives in Christianity: The Growth, Gifts and Diversities of Indigenous African Churches: A Challenge to the Ecumenical Movement* by John Pobee and Gabriel Ositelu II (World Council of Churches, 1998). *Christianity Made in Japan: A Study of Indigenous Movements* by Mark Mullins (University of Hawaii, 1998) introduces new Japanese Christian movements.

An overview of cultural issues in mission is pro-vided by Louis Luzbetak in *The Church and Cultures: New Perspectives in Missiological Anthropology* (Orbis, 1988). Robert Schreiter's *Constructing Local Theologies* (Orbis, 1985) is an influential discussion of how the gospel takes root in cultures.

A personal as well as theological perspective on Christianity's relationship with other religions is offered by Diana Eck in *Encountering God: A Spiritual Journey from Bozeman to Banaras* (Beacon, 1993). Kenneth Cracknell offers a historical perspective on Christian attitudes toward other religions in *Justice, Courtesy and Love: Theologians and Missionaries Encountering World Religions, 1846-1914* (Epworth,

1995). Raimundo Panikkar's *The Unknown Christ of Hinduism: Towards an Ecumenical Christophany* (Orbis, 1981) is a well known inclusivist perspective. Paul Knitter's pluralist review of historic stances is *No Other Name? A Critical Survey of Christian Attitudes Toward the World Religions* (Orbis, 1985).

Questions for Group Discussion

~ **Chapter 1: Dilemma and Discernment in Mission Today**

1. If your congregation has a mission statement, read through it together at this first session. What important connections do you see between your own parish mission and "missionary work" as defined in this chapter? If your congregation does not have a mission statement, spend some time talking about words that might express your church's sense of mission.

2. In this first chapter the author gives us some working definitions of what true mission might be, including its links with evangelism, outreach, and education. He also states that people often have misconceptions about mission. What ideas about mission did you grow up with? How do Presler's definitions and responses to some common questions affect your view of mission?

~ **Chapter 2: The Missionary God in Scripture**

1. In this chapter the author discusses Holy Scripture as a touchstone for Christian mission. He describes (in

relation to Genesis 1 and 2) God as being "busy on an errand." How does this unusual image of God strike you? If this is true and God really is "the first missionary," how does that change your view of mission?

2. Presler states that "spiritual discernment, not a to-do list for the world" should be the first step in planning mission. Discuss the ways that corporate prayer and discernment might enrich or alter your own "to-do" list for the planet.

∽ Chapter 3: Mission in History

1. Here Presler stresses that the "religiously diverse" world in which we find ourselves is not a new environment for the gospel, for the gospel first emerged in a society with many religions existing side-by-side. Discuss this in the light of your own city, town, or community. How religiously diverse is it? In what ways do these religious bodies undertake mission, either separately or together?

2. This chapter describes the distortions of Christian mission that can occur when it is coupled with the authority of the state, beginning with the emperor Constantine and continuing down to our own day. Think about the relationship between politics and religion in America, despite the separation of church and state. What distortions do you see?

∽ Chapter 4: The Anglican and Episcopal Mission Story

1. This chapter begins by evoking the statues of Westminster Abbey as important symbols of mission throughout history. Is your parish named after a saint, such as Peter or Paul, or an important doctrine,

such as Trinity or Incarnation? How does your church name inform its special mission calling?

2. Spend some time reflecting on your own parish's history, and ask the people who have been there the longest to describe some of the mission efforts of the past fifty years. Which have died out and which have flourished? Why?

∾ Chapter 5: Christian Mission and Other Religions

1. This chapter raises the very complex question of Christianity and other religions. Presler asks, "What basis is there for supposing that Christianity is a fuller or more valid way than other religions?" It is likely that everyone in your study group will have a different answer to this question, so make sure everyone has a chance to speak and to listen.

2. Turn to the two collects "For the Mission of the Church" on page 257 of *The Book of Common Prayer* and read them aloud. Discuss the ways in which these collects illustrate the tensions between Christianity and other religions in this chapter. Do they seem to you exclusivistic, inclusivistic, or pluralistic? Why?

∾ Chapter 6: Mission in Many Cultures

1. Consider this situation. A small Episcopal church with an aging congregation rents its liturgical space and community rooms to a fast-growing Vietnamese Protestant congregation with considerable energy and vitality. On Ash Wednesday tensions arise in trying to coordinate the worship schedules of the two congregations: the Episcopal Ash Wednesday service needs to be moved from 7 P.M. to 6 P.M. because the Vietnamese congregation now uses the church every Wednesday

night at 7:30. The change in time brings such a flurry of complaints filled with subtle hints of mistrust and racism that the vestry wonders if they were right to invite the new congregation to share the building.

You may have run into similar situations in your congregation. How do you think congregations should handle these questions of culture, custom, ethnicity, and difference? How can such issues weaken or strengthen parish mission?

2. Try to describe the "culture" of your own congregation. Is it urban, suburban, or rural? Homogeneous or diverse? Do parishioners have different ages, backgrounds, and education, or do they tend to resemble one another? What are some of the distinctive ways in which members of your congregation interact with each other and with people in the larger community? How might the gospel challenge the culture of your congregation?

~ Chapter 7: A Vision for Mission in the Twenty-First Century

1. Read together the ten marks or qualities of mission found at the beginning of this chapter. Which two or three best characterize the mission work in your congregation? Why?

2. Go back to the same list and select two or three qualities that seem to present a special challenge to your local community. Are there others you would like to encourage and develop in the future? In what ways could efforts in these areas enliven or change the focus of your parish outreach?

～ Chapter 8: Energizing Communities for Mission

1. Imagine that your study group is the newly formed Mission Committee in your congregation. Begin your initial session by sharing your backgrounds and particular interests in mission. Then turn to study the Bible, focusing on the call of Abraham (Genesis 12:1-9), Jesus' proclamation of his mission in the synagogue (Luke 4:16-30), or Jesus' encounter with the Syrophoenician woman (Mark 7:24-30).

Discuss some of the ways you might learn more about mission and missionaries, how you could raise up questions of mission in your programs of worship and education, and how your work as a committee could further the mission initiatives already in place in your congregation or diocese. End your "meeting" with intercessory prayer for mission, using the *Anglican Cycle of Prayer.*

2. Most of the dioceses in the Episcopal Church have a companion diocese relationship in another part of the Anglican Communion. Does your diocese have one? If so, how does that relationship affect the life and mission of the diocese? Does your congregation have a companion relationship with another congregation? If so, how does it affect the life and mission of your congregation? How could your congregation participate more deeply in this mission relationship? If your diocese or congregation does not have a companion relationship, why has it chosen not to take that mission approach? What could you do to encourage the formation of such a relationship?

Cowley Publications is a ministry of the Society of St. John the Evangelist, a religious community for men in the Episcopal Church. Emerging from the Society's tradition of prayer, theological reflection, and diversity of mission, the press is centered in the rich heritage of the Anglican Communion.

Cowley Publications seeks to provide books, audio cassettes, and other resources for the ongoing theological exploration and spiritual development of the Episcopal Church and others in the body of Christ. To this end, it is dedicated to developing a new generation of theological writers, encouraging them to produce timely, creative, and stimulating publications of excellence, and making these publications available widely, reaching both clergy and lay persons.